RELATIONSHIP COMMUNICATION AND NO MORE CODEPENDENCY

2-in-1 Book

Healthy Detachment Strategies To Resolve Any Conflict With Your Partner And Stop Struggling With Codependent Relationships

RELATIONSHIP COMMUNICATION

Mistakes Every Couple Makes & How to Fix Them. Discover How to Resolve Any Conflict with Your Partner & Create Deeper Intimacy in Your Relationship

Table of Contents

Introduction

Remember the first time you laid eyes on your significant other? It might not have been love at first sight, and maybe not even second sight, but I'm willing to bet on one thing: you thought winning them over would be the biggest challenge. You wanted so badly to get that date and when you finally succeeded in getting it, you wondered what you could do to get them to really like you. Now, months or years down the road, just when you thought it would all be smooth-sailing, you've found the puzzle only gets more confusing. Now, you realize winning them over was the easy part. Coexisting happily? That's a whole different ballpark.

Communication was simple when it was all sweet nothings and getting to know each other. Now that you're closer, there are different things on your mind. You have concerns, you have unmet needs, and you've noticed other ways you'd like to improve your relationship. Chances are that your significant other feels exactly the same way.

The problem is that these concerns are never easy things to express. If done incorrectly, it could hurt your partner's feelings and do irreparable damage. And yet if you don't express yourself, you just might explode, also doing irreparable damage. You're feeling a little cornered, aren't you? I don't blame you.

Your mind is probably swirling with a million questions like, "How can I communicate with my partner in the most effective way possible? How can I go about maintaining my happiness as well as his or her happiness? And how on earth can I do all this without completely exhausting myself?"

Even if you have pretty good communication already, why stop there? Aim for the stars. Your relationship deserves it.

Studies have shown that poor communication is one of the major reasons why a relationship fails. Many of those relationships could have been saved if they had this guide in their lives. A relationship ended over bad communication is a relationship that could have been saved. We can all learn to communicate better, no matter how shy or ineffective we may be now. All we need are the right tools and motivation. The fact you're here now proves there's a high chance you already have the motivation. Good for you. Now all you need is the expert advice. That's where I come in.

I've spent key years of my life studying the way humans interact with each other – how to use each gesture or glance as a key to a person's true feelings and intentions. I've paid close attention to the way individuals communicate and I've unlocked the secrets to what succeeds, and what inevitably fails. By staying attuned to the needs of others, I've discovered little-known tricks that can instantly shift a tense dynamic to an open, loving one. I've gained my expertise by staying aware of what works and what doesn't. I've watched relationships deteriorate over poorly phrased sentences, and I've seen couples reignite their love with just a few words. I've tested my methods on couples on the brink, and I've watched them blossom into their best selves. Even today, couples I've worked with continue to thank me. You see, once you have the tools, you're set for life.

With my help, you and your partner are one-step closer to the fantasy you both share – the one where you can say anything to each other and solve absolutely any problem together. You may not know you share this fantasy, but you do. When communication is strained, both partners desperately wish it could be better. You may think they don't notice, but trust me, they notice as much as you do. With my help, you'll make great communication the new norm. You'll start a brand new chapter where you can look back and think, "I can't believe how far we've come!" This book will strengthen you and your partner as a team. And do you want to know something else? A great team can do absolutely anything together.

Don't let this opportunity for growth pass you by. I've known many couples to express deep regret when they know they didn't try as hard as they could have. They continue to be haunted by times they were offered good advice and they said, "Maybe later." Truth is, the longer you wait to make these changes, the more stuck you become in your old ways. The longer you communicate to your partner in the wrong way (or don't communicate at all), the more hurt and strain your relationship accumulates. How much longer before your love breaks under the weight of it?

Choose love and choose your partner, by saying 'yes' to better relationship communication skills. Your new, happier future together is so close – it starts on the next page! So what are you waiting for?

Chapter One - Relationships 101

If there's one topic that dominates music, literature, film, you name it, it's without a doubt our romantic relationships. Do you ever wonder why this is? Romantic love is certainly not the strongest emotion we feel, and new parents would argue it's not even the strongest form of love. So why then do we continue to write and make art about it? The answer is simple: it's because we still don't understand it.

Romance and relationships are some of the most puzzling aspects of our lives. Feelings of attraction can come on unexpectedly, causing confusion and taking over our rational minds. Sometimes we have these feelings when it makes no sense at all to feel them. Swept up in new, burning romances, people can behave unlike their true selves and lose sight of their better judgment. And when we get into relationships, we enter a whole new realm of emotional confusion.

There's a bit of a paradox, isn't there? We get to know our significant others very well, and at the same time, we become more aware of how much we don't know. They are the people we know best of all, and yet they can also be the biggest mysteries. We may know their emotional responses, their habits, their tics, but rarely do we know *why* they are this way. Better communication is how we eliminate this distance.

Before we dive in, let's take a quick pause and remember something profoundly important: two halves make a whole. For a relationship to succeed, two individuals need to hold up their side of the equation. This doesn't just mean taking turns washing the dishes or splitting the bill. It means doing the self-work to be a better partner. It means reflecting on your needs and wants, your behavior, and considering how to be better when you're confronted with your dysfunctions.

So let's go to step one. Remember when we mentioned reflecting on our needs? Before we can begin to communicate our needs and wants, we must first know what our basic needs are.

The Vital Needs Every Relationship Must Fulfill

As complicated as relationships may seem, our basic needs are fairly easy to categorize. For a relationship to thrive, there are five basic but very important needs that should be met for both partners. Please note these basic needs aren't the only needs we have, they are just the ones we all share. Each individual has unique needs, depending on their personality and background, but for simplicity's sake, we'll start with the basics.

You may encounter certain personalities that have a higher tolerance for the lack of one of these needs. For example, have you ever met a boring couple that seemed just fine, despite their lack of variety? Or a couple that stimulated each other intellectually, but didn't have a true emotional connection? Many couples can make it work without taking care of all five needs. But the big questions remain: are they truly happy? Couldn't they be happier?

The Need to Feel and Be Secure

Without this need, a relationship is nothing. It's the most basic of the five and it refers to our deep need to feel emotionally, physically, and psychologically intact. If your significant other claims this need is not being met, serious work needs to be done. Feeling a lack of security could indicate a few types of problems: our physical well-being is threatened or we are being emotionally abused on some level. It all comes down to one partner feeling hurt and anticipating being hurt again, sometimes going through huge lengths to avoid it.

Many people don't realize this need is unmet because they think abuse is always intentional. This isn't true at all. Many partners don't realize they're using emotionally abusive tactics such as gaslighting or manipulation. They may have these responses wired into their brain without realizing how much damage it does.

When your need to feel secure isn't being met...

You feel like you can't be vulnerable around your partner. You fear they may verbally or physically hurt you if things don't go their way. You worry that instead of being met with love, you'll encounter more pain or distress. You constantly think of how they are going to react in response to something you do or say; this prevents you from expressing what you need to express. You fear that if you're honest about how you feel, you will be dismissed, mocked, or you might incite anger. You get the distinct feeling that if you share your needs, you will receive a negative response.

The Need to Feel Significant

Let's clear up a misconception: security and significance are not the same things. You may have total confidence that your partner won't hurt you, but is this enough to feel valued and special? It shouldn't be. Giving someone security is common decency, but showing them they're significant is a loving act. When our partner makes us feel significant and special, we feel good about ourselves and are overcome with warmth, knowing everything we give them is appreciated. We feel like the love we give is being received, and not just draining through a bottomless pit. This, in turn, encourages us to show even more love.

A person who has been cheated on is an example of someone who has had their need for significance compromised. There's no worse way to show someone they aren't special than by getting involved with another person behind their back.

When we get into a fight, we can continue to show our partners they're special by apologizing when we do something wrong. This shows we considered their feelings, tried to see their point of view, and are trying to make up for our wrongdoing. Show your partner love and appreciation. Otherwise, what's the point?

Make your partner feel significant by showing them love, and responding to their loving gestures with appreciation and affection.

When your need to feel significant isn't being met...

You find yourself worrying about your partner's infidelity or whether they truly love you. You may start to feel disposable, like your partner doesn't really see you for who you are. You don't feel particularly special in your partner's life. You feel like you serve a function, and not much more than that. You find yourself overcome by the feeling that you've given them everything, yet it's still somehow not enough.

The Need for Variety

When we get to know someone extremely well, our lives begin to form a routine. This is a normal occurrence, and unfortunately, the boredom that arises from it is normal too. To keep a relationship healthy and both partners happy, it's vital that we switch things up every once in a while. Studies have shown that we feel closer to our partners when engage in stimulating activities together.

This could mean anything: going out for dinner instead of cooking, signing up for a fun activity instead of staying home, or even doing something new in the bedroom. Whatever is part of your normal routine, do something completely different.

When both partners have busy work or family lives, a routine is inevitable. But it's completely within your power to make sure it doesn't become boring. Reignite the fire by adding a little more adventure!

When your need for variety isn't being met...

You don't feel as excited by your partner as you used to. It feels like you're stuck in a loop. It feels like your life together is just a series of tasks that need to get finished. It's been a while since you experienced a rush or a thrill together. A part of you longs to feel what you felt at the beginning of your relationship.

The Need for Emotional Connection

13

If a relationship is going to make it long-term, emotional intimacy is profoundly important. To maintain any close relationship in our lives, we need to make time to connect and allow ourselves to relate to each other. Sometimes this can come very easily to two people, but it's also completely normal for some couples to have to try a little harder. This doesn't mean you're any less meant for each other. Cultural, background, or personality differences can all be contributing factors to two people being more reticent. Start by sharing something honest and vulnerable, and invite your partner to share something similar.

When your need for emotional connection isn't being met...

Your partner sometimes seems like a mystery and there are times it feels like you don't really know them. You get the distinct feeling they don't understand you, and you, too, find their actions puzzling and confusing. You spend a lot of time wondering about them and why they do what they do. You may also feel there's something they need to say, but they're resisting saying it. You also feel the urge to share and open up, but there's never quite enough time. It all gets swept up in another moment.

The Need for Personal Expansion

If your relationship ticks the above four boxes, good for you. You've got a good relationship in your life. Want to know how to make it better? Give each other opportunities for expansion. In other words, help each other grow. Personal expansion can come in many forms, but essentially, we satisfy this need by feeling we've learned something or are learning something from one another.

In a healthy relationship, both partners encourage each other to be the best versions of themselves. They do not act complacent about their partner's goals or achievements, and they certainly do not put each other down. Give your partner positive, gentle feedback and constructive criticism.

Another way we fulfill this need is by stimulating our partner intellectually. Get into a discussion and teach each other new things. Expand each others' minds. Believe it or not, this all comes down to our biological need to procreate for further evolution. We want to find a partner we can truly collaborate with; someone who brings evolved qualities to the table or will evolve with us.

When your need for personal expansion isn't being met...

Your partner makes you feel stagnant. Sometimes you even wonder if they're holding you back from what you could truly accomplish. They don't inspire you in any way. When you get into discussions, it doesn't always feel like you're on the same page. You're often bored or confused by what they talk about. You don't think your partner is very wise or very smart.

The Five Stages of a Relationship

After studying hundreds of different couples, well-known relationship coach, Dr. Susan Campbell, noticed something interesting: just like human beings, relationships have their own lifetimes, made of five different stages. Each stage has its own distinct patterns and with a little self-awareness, all couples will be able to identify where exactly their relationship is.

Unlike with human beings, however, each stage will vary in length from couple to couple. And not every couple is lucky enough to learn the lessons of every single stage, especially the hardest stage of them all, Stage Two. To ensure you and your significant other power through these levels with love, trust, and grace, it's best to inform yourself on what they are.

STAGE ONE: Romance & Attraction

Of all the stages, this is the one you likely know most about. Hollywood films have convinced many people that stage one is what relationships are like all the time – but this could not be further from the truth. At this early point in the relationship, both partners are completely infatuated by each other. We still see each other through rose-tinted glasses, only seeing the positive aspects of our partner while in denial about their negative traits. Here, we still don't quite see our partners exactly as they are.

Your five needs are suspended in this stage because we are less likely to notice if they're not being fulfilled. We're more likely to shrug things off and give our partners the benefit of the doubt because the relationship is so new. We are very easily satisfied at this stage, choosing to see what we want to see.

The length of this stage varies wildly. Some couples progress to the next level after as little as two months and for some lucky couples, it can last up to two years – but rarely longer than that. Stage one generally lasts until partners decide to declare some sort of permanence. For some people, this is when they decide to start dating exclusively, and for others, it may be moving in together. How permanence is perceived varies from person to person.

STAGE TWO: Disillusionment & Struggle

After the euphoria and rush of stage one, we progress to the most difficult part of our relationship. This is when the rose-tinted glasses come off for the first time. We finally begin to see our partner and relationship as they are, and disappointment will begin to seep in. One or both partners will begin to long for how things were at the beginning of the relationship. This is where the balancing act comes in: how can we maintain our personal freedom while also being a good partner?

It's important to remember that going through this is completely normal. Because the media has given us such an unrealistic idea of love, we tend to jump to conclusions at the second stage. As soon as we encounter these problems, we think the relationship must be doomed. I'll tell you now: most problems that occur at this stage *can* be fixed!

To progress to the next stage, it's crucial that partners learn to:

- Accept each other for who they are and not who they want them to be.
- Come to an agreement and compromise about the behaviors and habits creating tension in the relationship.
- Acquire tools and strategies for positive self-transformation.
- Communicate honestly, kindly, and constructively.
- Embrace change and stop trying to fight it.

All at once, our needs come into play. If a need isn't being met, this is where we begin to feel that something is wrong. And if we're at all self-aware, we'll know exactly what this need is. Solving unmet needs now is the key to meeting them long-term.

Most divorces and break-ups happen during this period. It can last months or sometimes even years. Couples can be together for a long time and remain stuck in this stage, unhappy until they finally decide to part. Individuals are tested at this stage. How we choose to act and treat each other will determine the course our relationship takes. If we reject the lessons we need to learn, these problems may surface again in the next relationship.

STAGE THREE: Stability & Mutual Respect

If you make it through the storm, congratulations. There's more peace and harmony in stage three. Here, relationships have matured in a big way and both partners, whether they realize it or not, are better versions of themselves. Strategies are used and compromises are respected. Instead of trying desperately to change your partner, you focus on what's in your control. Let's use an example:

At stage two, Sam and Diane were constantly fighting. Diane would come home from work and see him sprawled in front of the sofa, watching violent TV shows and with an array of junk food spread out on the coffee table. This was his after-work routine. Sam wanted to relax and feel at home, but Diane wanted things to be cleaner and more organized. In their fights, Sam called Diane too strict and controlling, and she called him a messy slob.

At stage three, Sam and Diane have accepted each other's different needs. Diane now understands that Sam needs to let loose in order to de-stress from work. Sam also understands that Diane needs to see a clean and quiet environment to de-stress from her own job. The solution? On some nights, Sam can unwind how he wants, but he puts the TV volume lower so Diane can use a meditation app in the next room. Other nights, Diane can read in peace and quiet, while Sam watches his TV shows using headphones in the next room. And on special nights, they'll watch a show they both want to see and get snacks they both enjoy. If anything bothers them, they'll bring it up gently and kindly, without putting the other person down.

In stage three, you've decided to compromise and you are now adjusting to life with these new changes implemented. You are finally beginning to understand what makes a good partner. You no longer see compromises as infringements on your personal freedom, instead, you see them as opportunities for cooperation. All conflicts that arise are dealt with maturely.

The needs for emotional connection and personal growth are likely well-met during this stage. To avoid becoming bored and stagnant, make sure there's a healthy dose of variety.

STAGE FOUR: Love & Commitment

Here, love is fully-formed. All our actions spell out our commitment to our significant other. Not only have you accepted each other and learned to compromise, you've accepted your life together as *your life*.

This doesn't always mean marriage, but it is here that two partners are truly ready for marriage. In stage three, we accept our partner's idiosyncrasies, but in stage four, we love and embrace these differences.

Couples will still experience tension and conflict in this stage, but this is usually circumstantial or incited by new life events. Here, they've already worked out a dynamic for the situations they know well, but inevitably, situations they're not prepared for arise.

For example, Sam and Diane no longer get into heated arguments about how to behave at home. However, one evening at a dinner party, Sam told a story about Diane that really embarrassed her. He thought it would be funny but she argued it was too personal. Conflict like this is bound to arise sometimes, but using the tools they've learned in Stage Two, they can come to a resolution.

At this stage, it's important that partners make sure their needs for variety and emotional connection are met. The commitment has been solidified and sometimes this can mean the routine has begun to control their life.

STAGE FIVE: Symbiosis & Sharing

When we reach the final stage of our relationship, we are no longer insular and contained. Here, we begin to work together to give back something to the world. Once a strong foundation has been built, it's natural to want to build upwards and outwards.

This can mean children, but not for every couple. It can also mean starting a project or business. You know a couple is in this stage when they have a giving, almost parental quality to them or they just seem to *get things done* together. It's the opposite of two young lovebirds locking themselves in a room and not talking to anyone; a solid couple wants to share with the world in some form. They are ready to collaborate in every way.

Chapter Two - The Diagnosis

Think of the last time you went to the doctor. It doesn't matter what it was for, whether it was serious or completely mild, every single time you've had to be surveyed for a diagnosis. Before any solutions can be arrived at or any treatment administered, the symptoms must be noted and analyzed. It doesn't matter how potent the medicine is; if it's treating an ailment you don't have, it won't fix what's really wrong with you.

This same principle applies here. You can read up on great relationship advice, but not all of it will be helpful for your specific situation. If you want to improve your relationship, you're going to need to get real about what the issues are. The following chapter will focus on identifying your relationship's problem points. Be honest with yourself. The signs are there, you just need to notice them.

6 Big Signs You and Your Partner Need to Communicate Better

1. You talk about your partner more than you talk to them

It's completely normal to discuss our relationship with our friends and family, especially when we need advice, but consider this important question: do you ever share these same issues directly with your partner? How much do your communications *about* your partner outweigh your communications *with* them?

2. You've become irritable around your partner or vice versa

At one point in your relationship, it seemed like your partner could do anything and you'd let it blow past you. But now, it takes a lot less for you to lose your patience with them. You find yourself becoming irritated over small things that never used to bother you before. This is a key sign one of your needs is not being met, and a warning sign that you need to open up about it before you snap. Be honest with yourself and consider the real reason behind your lowered tolerance.

3. You find yourself wondering what your partner is truly feeling

We should never feel like our partner is a total mystery. If you frequently find yourself trying to figure out your partner like they're a complicated puzzle, then there's a lot that needs to be cleared up between you two. In a healthy relationship with great communication, we're on the same page as our partners 99% of the time.

4. You and/or your partner are prone to stonewalling

When one partner shuts down, refuses to be vulnerable and cooperate, this is called stonewalling. This goes deeper than the silent treatment. Someone who is stonewalling you will still speak to you, but you'll get the distinct feeling they have their guard up. They're not being real and they may even be playing games. A person who stonewalls is not communicating something that needs to be shared. Why else would they have such a strong reaction to being vulnerable?

5. You avoid certain topics and feel like you're walking on eggshells

Sometimes there is more than one elephant in the room. Sometimes it may even feel more like a mammoth. Does the room feel heavy with words unsaid? Is there noticeable tension? This is a big sign that the relationship is struggling with open communication. For some reason, neither partner is comfortable just saying what needs to be said. And chances are, this isn't the only thing they're struggling to say.

6. One or both partners is being passive-aggressive

Passive-aggression is a big sign that something needs to be said. It occurs when someone does not want to be obnoxious or outright aggressive, so they try to air their grievances without being completely upfront. They're not really being honest, they are trying to talk about it without *really* talking about it. Sarcasm is another form of passive-aggression when it is used in a nasty way. Whenever we can't communicate directly, we find more indirect ways of making our feelings known.

The Reasons Why We Don't Communicate

Knowing the reason behind poor communication won't give us the tools we need, but it'll show us where to begin working. How can we expect to get anywhere if we don't know where to start?

- **One or both partners has trouble being vulnerable**

This is a common reason why people don't communicate and it is an obstacle that can be overcome with practice. There are many extremely valid reasons why someone may have trouble being vulnerable. Sometimes there's a history of abuse, cultural differences, an oppressive upbringing, or maybe it's just that person's personality.

- **You're scared of being criticized**

When we're in a relationship with a highly critical person, this can affect our ability to be open with them. We're less likely to be honest because we'll constantly be thinking about how they'll react to our honest thoughts. Even if it's something that won't upset them at all, we may over-anticipate this reaction out of anxiety. It's important that the critical partner is identified in this scenario.

- **You don't realize there's something you need to say**

Many people in the world have been taught to live with a 'get up and move on' sort of attitude. While this is a great way to approach life's problems, it can cause communication to suffer in a relationship. Why? Because this attitude gets us in the habit of just swallowing our pain and distress, without acknowledging it. We try to suppress these feelings and in doing so, we become less self-aware about how we truly feel. So when there's something we desperately need to bring up with our partner, we may not be aware of what it really is. This can result in a lot of backhanded and passive-aggressive behavior.

- **Your lives have become busy**

When we're busy, we don't just fail to communicate because we literally have less time to talk. Having less time with our partner means we also start to lose a sense of intimacy. They're not around so we are no longer able to feed our connection. When we feel distant from our partners, we are less likely to want to share something personal with them.

- **One of you is keeping a secret**

It's a possibility we don't like to consider, but it remains a potentiality for any couple. When we have something to hide, it can take a toll on communication as a whole. Subconsciously or fully consciously, the partner with the secret starts to keep their distance, knowing that it's the only way they can protect their secret. Often, their significant other will also sense that something is off, which only leads to greater distance and even worse communication. This secret is not always a betrayal like infidelity.

- **You're holding onto resentment**

When one partner is holding onto a grudge, they stop allowing themselves to connect with their significant other. The grudge could be over something silly or something huge, but it always has the same effect. Resentment is so strong it can almost feel like a third entity in the relationship. Even if we verbalize that we've forgiven our partner, as long as there's any ounce of resentment, this forgiveness is not entirely present. When we secretly or not-so-secretly hold a grudge, communication can feel strained or completely nonexistent. The partner on the receiving end will feel like there's a wall they can't get past.

The 10 Communication Mistakes You Don't Know You're Making

Another beginner's step to improving relationship communication is to look at what's impeding progress. Before we can even think about remedies and solutions, we need to identify what behavior absolutely needs to go. It's time to be honest with yourself.

1. You're refusing to be accountable for anything

When we're faced with a situation that distresses us, it's difficult to accept we played a part in making it happen. But the harsh reality is we usually do. When we're in a relationship, it is vital that we learn to take accountability for our part in a situation. Apologies don't mean anything if there isn't accountability to back it up. When we learn to own up to our actions, we create a safe space of honesty, vulnerability, and kindness in our relationship. It reinforces the idea that you're a team. Yes, you both played a part in creating an unfavorable circumstance, but most importantly, you can both work together to prevent it in the future. Don't treat your partner like the villain; treat them like your team member.

2. You're dismissing your partner's feelings

Here's a secret you likely already know: sometimes you're going to think your partner's feelings are ridiculous. Sometimes, you won't understand them at all and you may have the urge to just walk away. It's important to stress, however, that you should *never* walk away or shrug them off. Dismissing your partner's feelings can do a lot of damage. You need to understand that even if it doesn't mean anything to you, it could be causing your partner a lot of pain. When you dismiss your partner's feelings you're telling them you don't care about how they feel. This can create even deeper pain for them and ruin communication in your relationship.

3. You're using harsh or abusive language

You could be saying something completely reasonable, but if you're using abusive language or calling them names to make your point, you're doing yourself and your partner a disservice. When we use abusive language to convey a message, it is far less likely to be heard. No one wants to be scolded like a child or made to feel like a failure. The language and tone we use should encourage our partner to do better, not shame them for what they've done. As soon as we do this, we make it more likely for our partners to act out of fear, instead of empowerment and love. This type of behavior can ruin a relationship and in some cases, it can even traumatize the person on the receiving end. It is essential to fix this behavior as soon as it arises.

4. You're yelling and screaming

If you're raising your voice or yelling at your partner, you're killing all chances of seeing eye-to-eye. Just like using abusive language, this is the wrong way to deliver a message. It doesn't matter how rational that message is or how right you are; when you yell and scream, you make your message less powerful. The delivery of your message should encourage your partner to cooperate with you, not cower in fear. When we act with aggression, we increase the likelihood of our partner's reacting with defensiveness. As soon as we do this, we enter combat mode. Nothing gets solved when we are in combat mode.

5. You always concede and apologize

It's not always about being too aggressive, you can also be too submissive. If you find yourself constantly agreeing and apologizing even though you didn't do anything wrong, you're taking the easy way out. It's true that we should pick our battles and sometimes it's more important to swallow our ego instead of arguing, but this shouldn't be a common occurrence. If you find yourself constantly running into the same problem with your partner, it's time to stop backing down so easily. If you continue to take the blame, the problem will never get solved because you're not the person who's causing it. For the sake of the relationship, you need to tell your partner how they are creating the situation at hand. Help them see the opportunity to make things better.

6. You throw around absolutes

Throwing around words like 'always' or 'never' when you don't mean it literally can sometimes be detrimental to the situation at hand. For example, if you say to your partner, "You're always whining" or "You never help me with anything" this is likely not an accurate statement. If it's not literally true, it can come across as hurtful because you're exaggerating the problem. It's essential that you stick to the facts when you're bringing up a problem, and steer-clear of finger-pointing language.

7. You're being *too* honest

We always hear that we should never keep anything from our partner, but that's not entirely true. It is possible to be *too* honest and it can cause a great deal of damage. As a rule of thumb, it's usually a good idea to be honest about something that you *did,* but it's not always necessary to tell them everything you *think.* If you're planning on having lunch with an ex, you should absolutely be honest about this. But should you tell your partner you find one of their friends attractive? Definitely not. This type of honesty can hurt someone's feelings.

8. You're not allowing yourself to be vulnerable

It's normal to feel some resistance towards being vulnerable. After all, we're giving someone very personal information and it's natural to want to protect ourselves. But for a relationship to be healthy, it's vital that we learn to be vulnerable with our partner. All this means is we need to share how we feel in an honest and open manner. It means showing a side of ourselves that we don't normally show anyone. To truly achieve a sense of intimacy, we need to let people in. Avoid communicating enigmatically or using sarcasm and humor in serious situations.

9. You're expecting your partner to read your mind

This is a common reason why people get mad at each other and it's easily prevented. The frustration stems from the idea that our partners should just *know* when something is wrong, and they should just *know* what to do to fix it. This is not at all fair to your significant other. Of course your emotions and needs seem obvious to you. After all, you're the one feeling them! There are many reasons your partner wouldn't notice and most of them are not worth getting mad over. The fact of the matter is when you're not expecting someone to have a certain reaction, you're less likely to notice the signs. So give your partner a break and just be honest. Once you get the problem out of the way, you can start working on solutions.

10. You attack your partner and not the issue

When our significant others do something that bothers us, it can be tempting to start attacking their character, but we should never do this. Let's say they completely forgot to pick up groceries on the way home from work. As maddening as this can be, do not say, "You're so forgetful. You forget everything!" Even if they do have a tendency to forget, always focus on the issue at hand. Instead of calling them forgetful, bring up what's really inciting your anger in this specific situation, i.e. forgetting the groceries. Consider saying something like, "I really wish you'd try harder to remember these important errands. I would feel much better if we could share the task of picking up groceries." You could even offer a solution like creating a phone reminder. You could also take some accountability and add, "I should have texted you to remind you. I know you have a lot on your mind after work." When we attack our partner's character, this is a put-down. It can make them feel terrible about themselves and this isn't helpful in creating a solution.

How many of these problems and signs have you recognized in your relationship? The more that you resonate with, the more desperately your relationship needs better communication. And don't worry, most of this is completely fixable!

Chapter Three - Habits for Happiness

The power of baby steps is highly underrated. Just think about it – our lives are not made of big achievements and end-destinations. It's made of the smaller struggles, the day-to-day grind, and the little victories that accumulate into big victories.

One of the major ways we set ourselves up for failure is by focusing on the end result and not the small steps that get us there. For example, we may say we want to lose weight, but instead of creating achievable step-by-step goals like "Only have dessert once a week" or "Eat one salad every day," we'll create big goals like "Lose 5 lbs in one week" without a single method to help our progress.

The secret to achieving anything is this: create good habits that support your goal. Want fantastic communication in your relationship? It's probably not going to be excellent immediately. And progress will be slow if you don't plan smaller, achievable steps. If you want better communication, you'll need to create better communication habits. It starts with implementing one technique, then another, and learning to make these new tools part of your routine. To succeed, you need to reinvent your norms.

9 Communication Habits that Save Relationships

1. Check-in with each other every day

This act is so simple, yet so powerful. At least once per day, get an update on how your partner is doing. This doesn't always mean asking "How are you?" it can also mean asking how their day was when you see each other after work. If you remember your partner mentioning a difficult upcoming meeting, ask how that meeting went. By doing this, we show our significant other we care and that we are listening.

2. Learn to use "I feel/It feels" statements

When you start a statement with "I feel" it turns a potentially accusatory or assumptive statement into something more gentle. For the best possible outcome in any situation, especially when one partner is in a tender state, "I feel" statements are the best way to communicate with them. Notice the difference between these two statements:

- "You're not listening to me. You haven't heard anything I've said."
- "I feel like you're not listening to me. It feels like you haven't heard anything I've said."

Switch the emphasis from "you" to "I." Notice how this makes something that could be interpreted as accusatory or aggressive suddenly becomes an honest observation. You're not telling your partner how they acted; you are emphasizing how you are experiencing their actions. There's a big difference. This is harder to argue with because when we explain how we feel, we become vulnerable. Since we are just saying "it feels" that way, we give our partner the opportunity to say that's not what they meant. When we don't use "it feels," we corner our partner, making their cooperation less likely.

3. Reconsider what you deem 'unimportant'

This less-known tip is remarkably effective at transforming relationships. When our partner says something we don't think is that important, we fail to make one massive realization: it could be very important to them! Whenever you're about to say "That's nice, honey" or perhaps even ignoring what they say altogether, consider the positive impact a proper response would have. If your partner just got home from work and she mentions in passing that she made a new friend, do not just nod and say "Oh, cool." Say enthusiastically, "That's wonderful you made a new friend."

Want to know something else? If your partner shows enthusiasm, even if it's for something small, you must meet that enthusiasm with interest or at the very least, you must acknowledge it properly. If you're taking a walk and your partner says, "Oh look! What a pretty bird!" it's very likely that you don't really care about the pretty bird. But you should still never ignore your partner when they are excited about something. Say "I wonder what kind of bird that is" or just agree with them by saying, "That is a very pretty bird, indeed." You should respond at least once to their statement.

All of this creates a closer connection and allows your partner to feel truly significant. It diminishes feelings of being ignored and unnoticed. If your partner's need for significance is not being met, this is a habit you should implement into your daily communication.

4. Ask them questions about their interests

Get in the habit of asking your partner about topics or events that interest them. I don't just mean subjects that they sort-of think are interesting, but the topics that get them really excited, even if they're a little silly. If your partner is into celebrity gossip, ask them what their favorite celebrity is up to lately, or ask what they thought of the latest article about them.

Think of the last time you saw your partner's eyes light up when they were talking. That's a good place to start. When we get into the habit of doing this, we build a stronger connection with our partners. It makes them feel special because you not only remember what they love, but you care enough to let them talk about it. As they speak, show genuine enthusiasm for what they're saying.

5. Say at least one positive or encouraging thing to your partner every day

It doesn't have to be a long, drawn-out love letter; just say at least one positive thing to your partner daily, even if it's short and sweet. It can be anything, and it should be spoken with enthusiasm. You're also free to do this by text. Some ideas are:

31

- "You've been working so hard lately. You know, I really admire what a hard-worker you are."
- "I know you've been stressed out, but I think you're handling everything very well."
- "You look wonderful today."

If you can't think of anything, then why not a simple but heartfelt "I love you"? Pepper more positive statements into your daily communication with your partner and you'll find your entire dynamic instantly becomes more loving.

6. If you disagree, gently invite them to reflect

You can't avoid disagreements with your partner, but you *can* avoid turning them into full-blown arguments. Instead of "you should" or "you shouldn't" statements, encourage them to reflect. Don't push an idea on them, lead them to it.

Let's use an example. Kelly has planned a lunch date with a friend that has always put her down and been mean to her. Her partner, James, doesn't think it's a good idea for them to meet up. Instead of saying, "You shouldn't meet up with her," he chooses to incite reflection. He asks, "Do you think she'll behave the same way she did last time?" and "What do you think will be different this time?" James allows his opinion to be known by using "I" statements. He says, "I just worry that she'll be a bad friend, like she normally is. I don't like to see you upset."

Use questions to invite your partner to reflect, and if you must add your opinion, always use "I" statements.

7. Still say 'please' and 'thank you'

When we stop using our basic manners with someone, it's a troubling sign that we've started to take them for granted. Make sure that no matter what happens you are always in the habit of saying 'please' and 'thank you' at the appropriate moments. Even if you're in a bad mood, you should still say it. This is the most basic way to show appreciation for someone, and when we stop, we display a sense of entitlement. You may think your partner won't notice but they will, especially when they've put considerable effort into providing you with something. Always show appreciation for your partner's efforts and adhere to these basic good manners.

8. Engage in pillow talk

Even when both partners have busy schedules, there's no reason they can't enjoy a little pillow talk. After all, we all need to go to bed at some point! Pillow talk occurs at the end of the day, when couples are winding down in bed. It consists of intimate and relaxed conversation where both partners can share their thoughts. Couples can choose to cuddle or not, but physical contact tends to create a more loving atmosphere. If you're having a somewhat tense conversation, cuddling can reduce combativeness and increase the likelihood of cooperation. When couples get in the habit of engaging in pillow talk, they have a greater chance at keeping the intimacy and connection alive in their relationship.

9. Share openly with your partner

To create a greater sense of intimacy and connection, don't wait to be asked questions – just start sharing interesting parts of your day. Tell them about funny things that happened at work, or about that hilarious text your friend sent you. If you're upset by something that happened, be vulnerable and share it with them. Once you start doing this you create an environment where sharing and openness is not just welcome, but completely normal. This means your partner is more likely to share with you as well. When distance grows between two people, they tend to overthink how to make it better. The solution is simple: just start acting like there's no distance at all.

When you share openly with your partner, make sure there's an opening for them to share as well. Do not spend hours talking about just you and your day. Invite them to share things that are exciting or interesting in their life. Of course, some of us are naturally more talkative, and at times, we just can't help it. To ensure that there's an even exchange of conversation, consider the following technique:

All About the 80/20 Rule

If you normally do most of the talking or you sense your partner needs to get something off their chest, opt for the 80/20 rule. This technique is extremely easy and straightforward. When you're talking to your partner, aim to listen 80% of the time and only talk 20% of the time. Don't use this technique in every conversation with your partner, as it's not always appropriate and sometimes it's best to keep it at 50/50. Bring it into play only if your partner needs to express something, if you sense an argument coming on, or if you just want to practice being a better listener.

Measuring Your Happiness with the Magic Relationship Ratio

To better understand relationship happiness, psychologists studied a wide variety of couples by asking them to solve a conflict in 15 minutes. These conversations were taped and watched back nine years later. The same psychologists made predictions about which couples would stay together and which would divorce. Amazingly, a follow-up with the couples involved found that the psychologists were 90% accurate about their predictions!

This led them to their discovery of the Magic Ratio in relationships. They found the major difference between unhappy and happy couples involved the balance of positive and negative interactions during moments of conflict. In this case, a balance of these interactions is not an even split. The Magic Ratio is, in fact, 5:1.

What this means is that for every negative interaction, a healthy and happy couple will have five or more positive interactions to offset the negativity. Negative interactions can include things like eye-rolling, dismissiveness, defensiveness or criticism. And to counteract this, couples should engage in positive interactions like physical affection, well-meaning jokes, apologies, showing appreciation, asking well-intended questions, acceptance, and finding opportunities for agreement. The 5:1 ratio indicates that a couple is happy, healthy, and likely to stay together in the long-run, while a 1:1 ratio is common for couples that are already on the brink of divorce or a break-up.

If there's anything to take away from this ratio, it's that negativity does a great deal of damage! After all, it takes five whole positive interactions just to offset a single negative one. Always keep that in mind moving forward and take care to not let too much negativity seep into your everyday interactions. Think about the last time you were in conflict with your partner. How many instances of positivity and negativity did you both display?

Stop Freaking Out About these 6 "Problems"

When we get into a deep relationship, so much begins to change – naturally, this makes us worry. Sparks and butterflies are replaced by other feelings, and it isn't entirely clear if this is a good or bad thing. Does this mean you're no longer in love? Is your relationship doomed to fail? Stop worrying! More often than not, couples worry about something that is completely normal.

It's important that we eliminate the habit of freaking out. When we freak out, we are so caught up in the emotion that we don't consider an actual solution. And let me tell you, there *are* solutions. Here are some of the most common relationship problems and better yet, how you can fix them through communication.

1. **Your relationship isn't as exciting as it used to be**

Of all complaints and worries, this one is by far the most common. Ask every single long-term couple and they'll tell you the excitement from their early days has settled. The rush of a new experience has been replaced by a sense of familiarity and closeness. Don't freak out about this! You've found stability. Don't think of it as having lost something, but as entering a new phase. Your relationship has leveled up.

It's important to distinguish between a relationship that feels less exciting and one that has lost *all* excitement. If you're in the second camp, you've got a little more thinking to do. Either you and your partner have sunk too deep into a rigid routine, or you've lost feelings for one another. Chances are, it's just routine. You've stopped taking care of each others' needs for variety, emotional connection, and personal expansion. Consider having a heart-to-heart and scheduling a date night. Make the effort to spice up your routine. It's not as difficult as you think!

2. Sometimes you desperately want alone time

It's not just normal to want alone time, it's actually very healthy. It means you and your partner have avoided becoming codependent and this is vital for the health of a relationship. Craving solitude means you still value your independence and this is something to feel proud of, not worried about.

Telling your partner you need some time apart shouldn't be a difficult discussion. Be direct, be casual, and avoid turning it into a serious talk – making it seem overly serious will cause your partner to think they did something wrong. Just say, "I haven't had any time to myself in a while and I've always needed solitude to recharge. Can I see you after the weekend is over?" If your partner is less independent than you are, conclude with a plan for your next meeting, so they have something to look forward to. Learning to ask for time alone is a fantastic habit to pick up when you're entering a relationship. Ideally, both partners should be able to take time apart whenever they need, without worrying about the other person.

3. You caught your partner checking out someone else

The first time you catch your partner's eyes wandering elsewhere, it can be very distressing. It's okay to be taken aback, but you should realize this is a completely normal occurrence. Even the most committed partners will find other people attractive. Attraction towards other people says nothing about their feelings towards you. Think of the last time you saw someone you found attractive. It could have been someone who passed you on the street, or perhaps it was an attractive celebrity in a movie. Remember how your eyes were drawn to that person? It was automatic, but not fueled by any real emotion. Our brains are wired to enjoy looking at what we find attractive, but eye-candy is all it is unless we chase it.

If this is a rare occurrence, it's probably not worth bringing up with your partner. This will only make them feel embarrassed and awkward. It may even cause them to feel anxious if they are around someone they find attractive – leading to even more discomfort for everyone! I only recommend bringing it up if your partner does it continuously and in an overt or disrespectful way. If their eyes linger too long, or it causes them to stop paying attention to you, feel free to say, "Could you please not do that? It really bothers me." Be direct and clear. And remember, this is a very common problem.

4. You have very different interests

Ask every relationship or marriage coach, and they'll tell you there are some very healthy, happy couples with completely different interests. Sometimes even opposite interests. In some ways, this can be good for a couple. With different interests, it becomes easy to maintain your independence, something that is very good for long-term partners. When a couple has everything in common, they risk spending too much time together, becoming codependent and if they aren't careful, burning out the fire of their relationship. Embrace the fact that you have different interests. Reframe your perspective: you're not too different, you *complement* each other.

If having different interests means you rarely see each other, make sure to schedule at least two days a week where you can partake in the same activity. For example, you could watch a movie at home, go to the cinema, go out to a jazz bar, or a theater performance. You could even choose to learn a new skill together, like pottery or painting. Talk to each other and come to an agreement about a way you can both have fun together.

5. Sometimes your partner really annoys you

You know those moments, don't you? You look over at your partner and you wish they'd just shut up. Or you wish they'd just sit still and stop doing what they're doing. On bad days, you might even become irritated by silly things like how loud they're breathing or how they talk.

Believe it or not, this is normal too – as long as it's not persistent. If you find yourself feeling this way for days on end, there's a chance you've either lost feelings for this person or you're spending too much time together. But if it lasts for only a few or several hours, and then you find yourself returning to your feelings of affection, then you have nothing to worry about. You're just in a normal, long-term relationship! During your moments of annoyance, know that it's normal, and resist the urge to say something hurtful.

6. You don't have sex as much as you used to

Surveys have shown this worry as being one of the most common. Couples, at nearly every stage, have some level of concern that they aren't having sex as much as they should. Truth is, it's completely normal for sex to become less frequent over time. And it's normal for the frequency of sex to fluctuate, depending on what's happening in each person's life. Once the honeymoon phase is over, a relationship begins to settle, and that's totally okay! This does not mean your partner no longer desires you, and it certainly does not mean feelings have been lost. If you're still worried, then schedule a time when you and your partner can drop everything and focus on getting intimate. And try something new you haven't done before!

Chapter Four - Love in Every Way

Communication isn't just about what we say in words. Consider the words, "Oh sure, that would be lovely." You can say that with kindness, but you can also say it with sarcasm, or hesitance. The meaning of everything we say can change based on our tone of voice, facial expression, and the pacing of our speech. Everything we do communicates a message.

Whether we're conscious of it or not, our partner is picking up signals from the way we carry ourselves around them. If you're talking to them but keeping your eyes fixed to your phone, this tells them you're not really interested in the conversation. If your words ask them to open up, but your body is turned towards the TV, this makes your words seem insincere. If you're actively trying to be a better communicator, you must make sure everything you're doing matches the message you're trying to send.

In this chapter, we'll focus on the many ways we can show our partners love. I advise embracing as many expressions of love as you can. And you may be surprised what your partner responds most positively to.

All You Need to Know about Love Languages

Does it sometimes feel like you and your partner are speaking completely different languages? You just might be. Since renowned marriage counselor, Dr. Gary Chapman, identified the five major love languages, it changed the game for millions of relationships. It demystified relationship dynamics, communication, and overall, fueled a greater understanding between partners.

Every single person gives and receives love in a different way. How we do this determines the actions we find loving and the actions we use to express our love for someone else. The way that we naturally communicate love is called our love language. It's common to have more than one, but rarely do we have more than two dominant love languages.

Two partners who are unaware they have different love languages may feel totally confused by one another. They might even feel unloved and unappreciated, unsure of why their attempts to show love have gone unnoticed. To create a smooth exchange of love and appreciation, it is absolutely vital that couples understand their significant other's love language.

Verbal Affirmation

One of the most common love languages is verbal affirmation. This means we use our words to express love and appreciation. People with this love language feel the most loved when someone verbalizes their feelings, pays them compliments, and gives them lots of verbal encouragement. Here are some examples of verbal affirmation:

- If your partner is ready and noticeably trying to look good, say, "Wow, you look fantastic. You're irresistible in this dress."
- If it's a cozy night in and your partner chooses a great movie to watch, say, "You always know just the right movie to pick. You have great taste."
- If your partner does something considerate, say, "This is so wonderful of you. Thank you. I really appreciate that you went through all this trouble for me."

If this is your partner's love language, pay attention to what they say in words. Do not disregard the kind and loving things they say, as this is how they are expressing love for you. Respond to these loving remarks with verbal appreciation.

Quality Time

Another way we communicate love is by giving our loved ones our undivided attention. Those with this primary love language need to feel a sense of togetherness and intimacy. They feel most loved when their partners make time especially for them and give them their complete focus. This isn't just about sitting together and watching a Netflix show, this is about bonding. Vulnerability is a huge plus for people with this love language. Your actions should send the message: "This time is just for you and I. Right now, I want nothing more than to feel close to you."

To communicate love through quality time, all you need to do is schedule a block of time where you can devote all your attention to your partner, and nothing or no one else. This could be a day at the amusement park, a special date night, or a getaway to a romantic place. It could even be as simple as staying in and sharing your days with each other over their favorite wine. Whatever you do, pay attention and listen carefully.

Physical Touch

If you're a very physically affectionate person, it's possible that you prefer to give and receive love through physical touch. A lot can be expressed in the way we touch someone. And as humans, we are wired to respond positively to it. If your partner's love language is physical touch, get used to making loving physical contact. To make your partner feel loved, make sure you hold hands, cuddle, kiss, hug, and nuzzle. People with this love language may also enjoy more sexual intercourse than other people, but this is not always the case.

The best part about this love language is that physical contact is so easy. You don't need much creativity or thought to communicate through touch. When you're passing through the room they're in, give them a peck on the cheek or rub their arm gently. When greeting them or saying goodbye, give them a warm embrace.

Acts of Service

If actions mean everything to you, it's possible you receive and give love through acts of service. When this is your love language, you feel most loved when your partner does something you want them to do. This is not at all about being a slave to your partner's every whim, it's about being thoughtful and doing something they didn't ask you to do. If this is your partner's love language, you should take some time to really think about what they'd appreciate the most. Make some aspect of their day easier on them. For example, you could cook your partner a meal they enjoy or fix one of their broken belongings. It could even be as simple as plugging in their phone if you see the battery is low. Perform actions that actively take care of your partner.

Gift Giving

If your love language is gift-giving, this doesn't mean you're a materialistic person. A gift is just physical proof that you've been thinking about someone. It doesn't need to be fancy or expensive. In fact, it doesn't need to cost anything at all. It's just about putting your loving thoughts and intentions into securing a physical object. It's not about the gift itself, it's about the thought behind it. Get used to giving gifts if this is your partner's love language. If they love chocolate, get a box or bar on your way home from work. If their favorite flowers are in bloom, pick up just one or a whole bouquet. And make sure to treat gift-giving holidays seriously!

How to Use Nonverbal Communication to your Advantage

As we established earlier on in the chapter, your partner is paying attention to everything you're saying, even the things you're not saying in words. To get the best outcome from a conversation, or to soothe them when they are feeling tender, follow these simple but effective nonverbal techniques:

- **Touch your partner in a supportive way**

Don't underestimate the power of touch. Putting an arm around your partner or holding their hand while they talk can make them feel much more at ease. A common tactic couples use when trying to come to an agreement is to cuddle or hold each other in some way, as they talk. Affection and touch can make individuals much more likely to cooperate with each other. Please note, however, that you shouldn't touch your partner if they are extremely angry with you – this can come across as inappropriate and make the situation worse.

- **Keep your facial expression neutral or sympathetic**

When you're listening to your partner speak, make sure your facial expression doesn't discourage them from speaking. If you're in a good mood, keep it sympathetic, and if you're not in a good mood, just keep it neutral. Even if we're upset with our partners, it's important that they feel they can speak without being judged. We may not be saying harsh words, but our facial expressions can still communicate an upsetting message.

Consider this scenario as an example: you're sitting with your partner, explaining to them how you feel very ignored when they're constantly on the phone during your date nights. How would you feel if your partner started looking at you with a raised eyebrow? What if they started scowling? What if it looked like they were about to laugh? Chances are you wouldn't want to continue sharing. And there's even a high likelihood you'd start to feel hesitant about sharing in the future. See? Even when we're not speaking, we're sending a message. Soften your features for a better response.

- **Turn your body towards your partner**

When you're speaking to your partner, especially about something serious, don't simply glance sideways at them. Make sure your entire body is angled towards them. When our bodies are turned away from the person we're speaking to, we send the message that we're not really interested in the conversation at hand. We show we're not truly invested. If your partner is upset or you sense they need some TLC, use your body to face them squarely.

- **Adjust the tone and sound of your voice**

It's not always about what you say, it's also about how you say it. Consider, in the moment, what your partner most needs from you. Do they need to just listen and empathize? If so, speak in a softer, more gentle voice. Do they need reassurance? If so, then speak with a firm, confident voice to make them feel secure. To soothe your significant other, speak slowly as a fast voice can come across as being dismissive.

Less-Known but Powerful Ways to Show Your Partner Love

Showing our significant other love in one or two forms just won't cut it. Why stop there? Whenever you get the chance, take the opportunity to shower them in warmth and positivity. This isn't just limited to the methods I've listed so far. The ways we can engage in loving behavior are endless.

1. Publicly declare how proud you are of them

It doesn't matter who you say it to; when an appropriate time comes up, why don't you proudly share one of your partner's achievements? It doesn't have to be a huge accomplishment, it can be anything that they worked hard on. Recognize your partner's efforts and share their achievement with an outside party. Everyone is taught to stay humble and never brag about their successes, but sometimes we secretly want people to know we succeeded at something. Be the first to share something amazing your partner did. It'll make them feel extremely loved, supported, and they'll likely feel encouraged to keep making progress. This tactic might make them blush at first, but once the shyness wears off, they'll feel very touched.

2. Stand up for your significant other

If something unfair happens to your partner, don't be afraid of speaking up. This doesn't mean you should start a fight or say something nasty, it simply means you should vocalize your support during a difficult situation. Use your common sense to determine the right way to do this. If you're in a conversation with lots of people and someone puts your partner down, counter it by acting as their cheerleader.

Consider this example: Adam and Vanessa are out with a group of friends. Someone starts making fun of Vanessa because she mentioned she was writing a novel. The rude person remarks on how everyone else is working a high-paying corporate job while Vanessa is at home writing stories. Adam doesn't need to start a fight to stand up for her. All he says is, "Writing a novel takes a lot of patience and determination. Vanessa has been working very hard and I think it's wonderful that she's chasing her passion instead of becoming money-obsessed." No negativity required!

3. Make an effort to bond with the people close to them

It's true what they say; when you start dating someone, you date their close friends and family as well. Whether you like it or not, these people are here to stay. And if you don't make the effort to leave a positive impression, their opinions could have an influence on the course of your relationship. When you get to know your partner's close connections, you send the message that you really want to be a part of your loved one's life. You demonstrate you're serious, and you display genuine love. Why? Because you're engaging in an entirely unselfish pursuit. After all, your partner's friends and family don't satisfy any of your needs and desires. Don't give in to the idea that they aren't important because they're not your partner. How you treat them speaks volumes about how you see your relationship.

4. Ask your partner what they enjoy in the bedroom

There's this unhealthy idea that we should all just *know* what our partners want, without ever asking them. Many people are under the mistaken impression that if we can't just figure it out on our own, we're not good in bed. This is a ridiculous notion. We're not mind-readers and every single person has different preferences. A lot of people are not forthcoming about what they like because they don't want to seem demanding, so why not just ask? How can we get it right if we never know?

Even if you already know what your partner likes, there's nothing wrong with having a check-in. Ask them if there's anything you did recently that they enjoyed, and ask them if there's anything you can do better. Learning to communicate openly about sex is one of the best things we can do in our relationships. It also shows our partner how devoted we are to making them happy and meeting their needs. Even if we don't always get it right, it can make the difference to know we're trying.

5. Learn more about a topic that interests them

If your partner is a huge science-fiction nerd, try and watch their favorite show or movie. If they love discussing politics but you don't understand it, ask them to explain something to you. Open up and expand your horizons! Show your partner you're really interested in what they care about. You never know, you may even find that you're interested in it as well. We should always try to create opportunities for bonding with our partner. By engaging with what interests them, we create more intimate moments. This is a sure way to strengthen your connection.

6. Take care of them when they're sick

It's fairly common for women to take on a nurturing role when their partners are sick, but unfortunately it's less common to see it happen the other way around. One of the most loving things we can do for our partners is to take care of them when they're at their weakest. This includes all types of physical and mental ailments, including sickness, depression, or even grief. This doesn't mean we have to wait on them hand and foot; it just means offering some strength when they need it the most. This loving gesture tells our partner that we care for them, even when they are too weak to offer us anything in return.

7. Make time to relive your love story

Every single couple has a unique love story. It encompasses all the wonderful, exciting things about a new romance: how you met, what you first thought of each other, when you knew you wanted to be with them, and so much more. A great way to continue reigniting love and passion is by actively reliving your love story with your partner. Why not revisit the place you had your first date? Or the place you had your first kiss? Or how about just tell each other your different sides of the story? When did you both know it was love? When a couple does this, they're taking a step back to remember why they're with each other. They are disconnecting from their current troubles and making the effort to not lose sight of the magic. We all have a love story; take the time to remember yours.

8. Make plans for the future

Alright, calm down, this doesn't mean you need to start planning your wedding or naming your future children. It just means you need to paint a future with your partner in it. It's not about committing to forever, it's about coming up with shared goals and creating shared dreams. Identify something you can both work towards achieving together. This creates a more hopeful and collaborative environment in the relationship. By doing this, we show our partner that they, too, are part of the dream and part of the goal. It is the positive kind of self-fulfilling prophecy, where we subconsciously do our best to thrive alongside our partner because we have a goal to reach for.

Chapter Five - Decoding Your Partner

A short message from the Author:

Hey! Sorry to interrupt. I just wanted to check in and ask if you're enjoying the *book title* audiobook? I'd love to hear your thoughts!

Many readers and listeners don't know how hard reviews are to come by, and how much they help an author.

So I would be incredibly thankful if you could take just 60 seconds to leave a quick review on Audible, even if it's just a sentence or two!

And don't worry, it won't interrupt this audiobook.

To do so, just click the 3 dots in the top right corner of your screen inside of your Audible app and hit the "Rate and Review" button.

This will take you to the "rate and review" page where you can enter your star rating and then write a sentence or two about the audiobook.

It's that simple!

I look forward to reading your review. Leave me a little message as I personally read every review!

Now I'll walk you through the process as you do it.

Just unlock your phone, click the 3 dots in the top right corner of your screen and hit the "Rate and Review" button.

Enter your star rating and that's it! That's all you need to do.

I'll give you another 10 seconds just to finish sharing your thoughts.

----- Wait 10 seconds -----

Thank you so much for taking the time to leave a short review on Audible.

I am very appreciative as your review truly makes a difference for me.

Now back to your scheduled programming.

In the early days of a romance, getting to know the person you're madly attracted to is an exciting pursuit. Everything about them is fascinating and almost spellbinding. Every new quirk you discover is adorable, even the objectively annoying ones. Their unique qualities draw you in and you're convinced there's no one like them in the world. Your feelings are on fire in the best way possible. You can't wait to fully unravel your partner and deeply get to know them in every single way.

Once things become serious, your attitude is likely to see a shift. This isn't a bad thing. In fact, it's extremely normal, as I've demonstrated in the first chapter. While you still love your partner and their unique quirks, you've also discovered the other dimensions to their personality, the sides that weren't apparent in the early days at all. Every person has a dark side. We all have inner conflicts, our own particular needs, and even when all our secrets are laid bare, there are bad days where we suddenly play to an entirely different tune. Like I mentioned, this is completely normal. This is human nature. This will happen in every relationship you encounter and to be a good partner, you need to learn to roll with it.

Your significant other may feel like a mystery at times, but he or she is far more simple than you think. It all comes down to the basic needs which we all share, and some unique needs which are entirely their own. You'll learn about them over time and gradually perfect how to take care of them. The process of decoding your partner takes awareness, understanding, and kindness, but it's one of the best things you can do for your relationship. This is what love is all about.

Understanding Your Partner's Particular Needs

With every single partner you're with, you're going to need to take the temperature on their various needs. Trouble is, 'needs' is such a vague term, and you may not be sure where to begin. If you want to make your partner happy, consider these different types of needs and make sure you understand your partner's preferences. This may take some intent observation, but you should also feel free to just openly discuss these topics with your partner. This way, there is no confusion at all.

● **Their sex drive and sexual needs**

It's true that our sex drives can fluctuate but some people just have a much higher sex drive than others, at all times. And there are also other people that just don't crave it as much. Assess your partner's needs or just straight-up ask your partner how high they would rate their sex drive. You may find they have a similar sex drive to you, but you may also find you have differing needs. This means that later on you'll need to find a compromise so neither partner feels unsatisfied. You'll also need to discover what they specifically enjoy in the bedroom. Keep in mind that everyone's different and it may even be beneficial to just outright ask your partner what they like.

● **The way they destress and relax**

There are certainly common threads, but for the most part, we all have different ways of destressing and unwinding. For some people, this can mean total peace and quiet, eating healthy food, and taking a walk in the park. At the opposite extreme, some people like watching loud

TV, playing video games, and want nothing more than to gorge on greasy pizza. You'll even find that some people like to be social when they relax, and others like to be completely alone. It's always best to find out what your partner's needs are after a long day. Once you know, you can help create the right environment for them when you know they need it the most. It's also perfectly normal for people to have a few ways they like to destress, but you'll likely notice a pattern. If you and your partner have conflicting ways of destressing, make sure to find a way to compromise.

- **Their idea of adventure**

Adventure doesn't always mean skydiving or roller-coasters; our need for adventure arises when we have energy and are in the mood to do something fun. Maybe even something different from our usual routine. We're ready to exert energy, instead of trying to preserve it. A common idea of adventure in the modern day is going out for a night on the town, dancing, and having some delicious cocktails. But some people, even on their best days, don't want to do this at all. Some people like to be indoors and engaging in private activities. Perhaps, they want to cook or bake, or do a home work-out video. When it comes to adventure, we're much more likely to have many ideas of fun. In this case, it's best to note what your partner's favorite thing is, and to rule out what they definitely *do not* consider fun. It's important that whatever they like to do, you either learn to enjoy it too or just accept that they enjoy doing it.

- **Their needs for mental and intellectual stimulation**

To put it simply, what we find mentally and intellectually stimulating is what we find interesting. It encompasses all the topics that we enjoy feeling challenged by and exploring. This is one of the easiest needs to discover as people are more upfront about what mentally stimulates them. You just need to pay attention.

Some people choose to not classify this as a need, but I would beg to differ. When we are deprived of what we find interesting, our personalities wilt and we feel lackluster, perhaps even depressed. Those who stop engaging with topics they enjoy can even complain of feeling less like themselves. It's important, once we identify these stimulation needs in our partner, to always actively listen and participate as much as we can. What are the topics that bring your partner joy? When do you see their eyes come alive? Whatever these topics are, we must always allow our partner to bring them into the wider conversation. This is how we can help satisfy their need for personal expansion.

- **Their emotional support needs**

Inevitably, a time will arise when your partner needs emotional support. While their needs will vary with each circumstance, you'll notice there are patterns in what they find soothing during times of emotional hardship. For some people, it's important to cry, in which case you should make sure to be an understanding shoulder to cry on. Some people become more hungry and have more cravings during times of emotional stress, in which case, you should try to give them whatever food they find nourishing. There are even people who need to be completely alone to feel supported. They may just want to escape into nature by themselves and they'll need you to understand that. Whenever your partner is going through a time of hurt, try to learn what eases the pain. During these periods, it can also be a good idea to turn to the five love languages.

- **Their spiritual or religious needs**

If your partner doesn't adhere to any specific spiritual or religious practice, then there's no need to worry about this section. However, more often than not, we encounter people that have some shred of spirituality in their lives. Spirituality and religion is a highly personal matter, and it's highly important that we respect our partner's choices and beliefs. Even if it seems silly to us, it brings our partner peace and this is all that matters. Know what your partner's spiritual practices are, when they need to do it, and if there are any other requirements they need to abide by, such as dietary restrictions. We should never argue with their spiritual needs and we should never make fun of them.

- **Their insecurities and needs for reassurance**

You're never going to find a partner without any insecurities. That's just how it is. We're all human and we all have fears shaped by our backgrounds or personalities. It is absolutely vital that you understand what your partner's insecurities are. And most importantly, you must know how to prevent bringing those insecurities to the surface, and what they need from you when they do arise. For example, let's say your partner is insecure about his or her weight. This insecurity might be triggered when they meet someone very thin and attractive. These situations are unavoidable so it's best to come up with an action-plan for when it does happen. Perhaps, later on, you should try and tell your partner how sexy they are, and focus all your energy on making them feel attractive. Or perhaps, your partner would prefer to just forget it and do something that takes their mind off their body entirely. These needs will differ from person-to-person.

5 Absolutely Essential Things to Do When Your Partner Has Experienced Trauma

When you finally meet the person you want to be with, chances are they saw a heck of a lot before you came along. Sometimes even, a little too much. If your partner has been touched by trauma in their romantic or sexual encounters, you'll have to be more gentle with them. This is a non-negotiable. If we don't adjust our behavior, we will never make our partners happy, and we may end up causing more damage.

There are many types of trauma that can leave a painful and emotional scar, from cheating to emotional abuse, and in some cases, more physical kinds of abuse. Communication tactics should always be softened during specific scenarios to ensure you don't trigger them or cause them to withdraw. Always keep the following tips in mind if your partner has endured trauma:

1. Learn about the trauma in a non-intrusive manner

Before we know what to do, we must know what we are dealing with. The first step is to try and learn about the traumatic incident. Depending on the severity of the trauma, it may not be as simple as asking our partner what happened. If it is too painful to recount or they are just not ready to tell us, there are only two things we can do: wait for them to feel ready, or ask someone they are close to. A good first action is to tell your partner, "You don't have to tell me anything you don't want to, but I'm always here if you want to share. I just want to know how I can support you in the best way possible." Let them know you care about their past, are ready to listen, but that you won't push them to do anything they don't want to do. It's important that you never force or guilt-trip them in this situation.

2. Consider the types of behavior that may trigger their traumatic memories

This stage requires your deep thought. Think of the qualities and behavior that hurt them during this traumatic incident. Sometimes it's straightforward, such as physical violence, but not all the time. If your partner was cheated on, they may feel triggered by something as mild as you talking to members of the opposite sex. They may become anxious on the nights you go out drinking with your friends. If there are moments where you stop communicating, this could be especially hard for them as they might suspect you are keeping a secret. Identify the behavior involved in the traumatic incident, but also what may have led to it.

3. Decide on alternative or modified ways of behaving

It's not always realistic to eliminate every single behavior that could possibly trigger our partner. While it's easy (and absolutely necessary) to not abuse someone, it's not easy or realistic to completely stop talking to members of the opposite sex. So what can we do instead? It's simple: we must modify the way we engage in this behavior. For example, if you're texting a member of the opposite sex, you could consider letting your partner see the messages so they can ease their worries. If they become anxious when you're out drinking with buddies, consider having a check-in via phone call every couple of hours. Or send them a photo of you at your current location. Get creative about how you can modify your behavior without eliminating completely normal actions. And you should always feel free to simply ask your partner, "What can I do to make you feel better in this situation?"

4. Understand what they need if they are triggered

Hopefully this never happens, but if your partner's trauma is linked to common events, it may be inevitable. When this happens, you must be completely calm and gentle with your partner. If you are angry with them for some reason, you must put this on hold until they've stopped feeling overwhelmed. Otherwise, this will only exacerbate the situation.

How this situation manifests will vary with each person, but the most common response is either crying or going into self-defense mode, as if the trauma is happening again and they must protect themselves. The best thing to do is to offer reassurance and take on a soothing tone of voice. If your partner was a victim of violence, play it safe and do not touch them at all until they are ready. Understand that sometimes our partners may not have obvious signs of being triggered. Instead, they may just become quiet and depressed. It's important to keep an eye out for less noticeable responses if you know they've been exposed to a potential trigger.

What each person needs depends highly on the person and the trauma they experienced. A good rule of thumb is to remove the trigger as soon as possible and do the opposite of what started it.

5. Know what you can do to help them move on

If the trauma is severe and very rarely comes up, then it's best to disregard this stage entirely. However, if the trauma is getting in the way of your relationship, or preventing your partner from advancing their life, think of ways to help them make more peace with what happened. This could mean seeking out professional help or coming up with step-by-step solutions amongst yourselves. It's important that these solutions are not just your responsibility; these steps should also challenge your partner to create more healthy response patterns.

Let's go back to the example of the jealous partner. It's not realistic to expect someone to call you every couple of hours every single time they go out drinking. Ideally, the jealous partner should move on from this behavior once the relationship starts to become more long-term. To start this positive transition, they could make calls less frequent during each night out, or they could decide to just text every hour. The jealous partner should come up with steps they can do to avoid feeling low or depressed during these incidents. Perhaps, they could also go out with friends or channel their energy into an intense work-out session. Create a positive new habit to take the place of unhealthy responses. This way, everyone wins.

Chapter Six - It's All About You

We're often told we should find a significant other that loves us as we are. This is true, to an extent. We should all expect our partners to love and accept us for our likes, dislikes, and our positive attributes without trying to change them. They should even love us for our quirks, flaws, and idiosyncrasies. They should love what makes us different. But no partner should ever be expected to put up with negative or destructive behavior that deeply affects them. Your arrogant attitude, your manipulative tendencies, your persistent laziness; none of this is your partner's responsibility and if it hurts them, you'd be cruel to ask them to accept it. Asking our partners to deal with what upsets them and hurts them will inevitably lead to contempt. And contempt is one of the few things a relationship cannot heal from.

The majority of relationships fail because one or both partners refuse to do the self-work. I urge you now to not be the partner that doesn't do the self-work. Don't be the one who doesn't make the effort. You may feel indignant now, but if the relationship ends and you know you didn't try your hardest, you're going to be left drowning in regret. Work on you, before it's too late.

And remember, it doesn't end here. The behavior that hurts your partner now will likely hurt all your future partners to come. As long as you want to be in a happy, healthy relationship, you will continue to need positive self-transformation.

How to Instantly Become a Better Partner

If you want to do right by your partner, implement these easy habits into your dynamic. Create these new communication norms and you'll instantly start to see better results in your relationship.

1. Ask for what you need

58

Stop expecting your significant other to read your mind. They have their own life, with their own needs, and you can't expect them to sit around trying to guess how you feel. Asking for what you need does not make you needy, it makes you self-aware and emotionally mature. It shows you value your relationship because you're serious about creating better conditions. Instead of expecting your partner to jump through hoops, you are being upfront about how to help. This makes it easy on them. This gives them a real opportunity to adjust their behavior.

When you ask for what you need, you are much more likely to *get* what you need. To get the best outcome from your discussion, remember to use "I feel" statements.

2. Bring up a problem before it gets worse

There are many reasons we avoid bringing up problems. Sometimes it's because we're uncomfortable with confrontation, afraid of the other person's response, or perhaps, we just don't want to admit there's a problem. What usually happens is the problem continues and gets worse. When we avoid bringing up our problems, we risk two things.

- Exploding at our partner when we just can't take it anymore. When we allow ourselves to reach our breaking point, we are more likely to say something harsh that we don't mean. This can upset our significant other and it may even cause lasting damage to the relationship.

- Developing contempt for our partner. If we don't give our partner the opportunity to make it better, it will not get better. This will frustrate us more and more, and eventually lead to resentment. You may find your mind swarming with questions like, "How on earth can he/she not notice? Why isn't he/she more aware of what this is doing to me?" This can spiral into feelings of not feeling cared for, and anger at your partner for putting you through this. Newsflash: you are putting *yourself* through this if you don't tell your partner what's wrong!

3. Pay attention to timing

Always consider the timing of what you do and say to your partner. This makes a massive difference in the response you receive from them. If you're trying to have a serious talk with them, don't do it when they're exhausted from work or if they've had a bad day. This could incite an argument since they're not in their right mind. Always use timing to your advantage. Talk to your partner the morning after they've had a night of great sleep or on a day they seem level-headed.

This rule extends even beyond serious talks and discussions. Whenever you're going to make any decision that impacts both you and your partner, think of where this will fall on their timeline and schedule. If there are days of the year that are particularly hard for your partner (for example, anniversaries of deaths), remember them. Ensure you don't plan any big social events when they would prefer to lay low.

4. Use gentle and constructive language

Mistakes happen. And sometimes our partners don't always have the greatest ideas. Still, you should always make the effort to stay constructive when providing your partner with any feedback. Acknowledge what they did right, but also point out opportunities for growth. If you feel the need to criticize your partner, always reframe your comments from the perspective of how they can improve. If you make them feel like everything they do is wrong, you're not fixing the situation, and you're only disempowering them from cooperating with you. Always focus on solutions.

5. Always listen, always

This one gets repeated a lot, but it's for a good reason. Active listening in our relationship is extremely important. In fact, it is directly linked to the overall quality of communication with our partner. And in an unhappy couple, it is highly common for at least one partner to complain that they don't feel heard and their significant other never listens to them. By listening, we are staying present in the conversation. We are showing our partner respect. And by actively listening, we are also lowering the likelihood of misunderstandings. The next time your partner is speaking, avoid just waiting for your turn to reply and really absorb everything they're saying.

6. Keep your expectations kind and realistic

We all move through life and make progress at different paces. This is no more true for you and your partner. One way you can cause needless disappointment for yourself and hurt for your partner is by expecting far too much from them. If it seems like you're always waiting for your partner to tick off boxes on your checklist, take a step back and re-examine the extent of what you're asking. If you find yourself continuously disappointed, consider why before taking any further action. Are you trying to change their personality? Are you asking for too big of an adjustment too fast? Are your demands being insensitive to their current life circumstances? These are all necessary questions to ask yourself.

Some specific examples of unfair expectations:

- Expecting your partner to be on top of all the chores when someone close to them has just passed away.
- Wanting your partner to become athletic because you are most attracted to athletic people.
- Expecting your partner to cook a wonderful meal and keep the house spotless after a stressful day at work.

- Demanding that your partner immediately become great at that move you like in bed, when they're already giving it their best effort.
- Expecting your partner to have all the same positive qualities as your previous partner.

Please note that these expectations do not apply to matters of compassion, respect, safety, consideration, and kindness. These do not count as high expectations, this is basic human decency. No matter what your partner is going through, they should always be meeting these basic expectations.

7. Stop bringing up the past

To clarify, it's not bringing up the past in itself that's damaging, it's when we dredge up the past to start an argument. If you've already talked about it and your partner has apologized, we shouldn't continue to hold their mistakes against them. If we do this, we're demonstrating we haven't truly forgiven them. As long as we continue to hold this grudge, we are creating negativity in the relationship. Either you should move past this mistake and forgive your partner, or if you can't forgive them, do what needs to be done and end the relationship. Continuing to throw past mistakes in our partner's face is a cruel act as it traps them in the mistake. Not only this, but it increases the likelihood of us getting into circuitous conversations that are never solved. Since we are so attached to the problem, we can never move onto solutions. Stop using the past as a weapon and try your best to move on, if you're deciding to stay.

8. Express gratitude more often

Science has proven that when we approach life with gratitude, we instantly feel happier. Not only does expressing gratitude in our relationships lead to our own happy feelings, but it can be transformative and powerful for our partners. By showing gratitude, we are reminding them of their tremendous worth and highlighting what they are doing right.

Being on the receiving end of gratitude can be incredibly empowering. If your partner is going through a hard time, it will ignite more motivation and progress, ultimately creating more satisfaction in the long run. But most importantly, it shows them that their efforts do not go unseen and that you recognize all they do. This will instantly make them feel more positive and valued. Gratitude is, overall, a big win for everyone. Express it more often! You'll be glad you did. It's as simple as telling your partner "I love you and appreciate you" or highlighting a specific action they did/do and explaining in more detail why you're so grateful for it.

Understanding Your Relationship Attachment Style

Our attachment styles are formed in early childhood and they play a major role in our relationships. According to psychoanalysts, the attachment style we form all comes down to the dynamic we had with our caregivers, during infancy. This style determines our behavior patterns, the types of relationships we're most likely to choose, and essentially how we go about getting our needs met.

No attachment style is 'bad' per se, but some are less conducive to harmonious relationships and more inclined to exhibit unhealthy behavior. In any case, it's always important that we're aware of our attachment style (and our partner's as well) so we can have a better understanding of our behavior patterns and responses.

- **The Anxious-Preoccupied Attachment Style**

Those with this style tend to crave emotional attachment and may have a history of tumultuous relationships. They tend to dislike being alone and are prone to fantasizing about their dream partner. Unfortunately, this attachment style encounters a lot of stressors in a relationship. A lot of these are self-inflicted. During times of emotional distress, they can become jealous, possessive, or needy. They require a lot of love and validation, and they may react negatively if they don't receive reassurance or positive reinforcement.

It can be said that these types live in their heads a lot. They are often their own worst enemy, intensely worried they'll be betrayed. Those with this attachment style make up about 20% of the population.

- **The Dismissive-Avoidant Attachment Style**

Quite the opposite of the Anxious type, the Dismissive-Avoidant is highly self-sufficient. This type displays a great amount of independence and requires a lot of freedom in their relationships. Though they may secretly desire a deep connection, they will appear closed-off and rarely engage deeply in relationships. Many people who date these types end up complaining that they seem emotionally unavailable and at times, even indifferent. It takes more work for them to show vulnerability, and some may even be commitment-phobic. They tend to see intimacy as a loss of their personal freedom.

Avoidant types are so accustomed to taking care of their own needs that they can become plagued by obsessions as a way to self-medicate. This may be substance abuse, or something less damaging like exercise or food. Roughly 23% of the population consists of these types.

- **The Fearful-Avoidant Attachment Style**

This type lives with a lot of conflict. A combination of the previous two styles, the Fearful-Avoidant exhibits a push-pull pattern of behavior. They deeply crave a close connection and yet part of them wants to run away to safety. Unfortunately, this type tends to do both those things. During their worst moments, they may cling to their partner and even appear quite needy. But once their partner gets close to them and comforts them, they may suddenly feel suffocated and trapped. Like Anxious types, the Fearful personalities are also prone to turbulent relationships.

These unpredictable types don't have a fixed strategy for meeting their needs. Their behavior patterns are often a result of trauma from abandonment or abuse. This is the most rare attachment style, making up only 1% of the population.

- **The Secure Attachment Style**

As its name suggests, this attachment style is the most secure of the four, and is widely considered the most emotionally healthy. They have higher levels of emotional intelligence and find it easier to regulate their emotions. Healthy boundaries are easy to set and they have a generally positive outlook on relationships. This type feels secure in a relationship, and they also do just fine on their own. Overall, they tend to be more satisfied in relationships and have a much easier time forming a healthy connection.

The Secure Attachment style is formed when one's childhood is experienced as mostly positive. Caregivers were perceived as secure and safe, so they continue to project this experience onto all future relationships. This is the most common type of all, with 57% of the population characterized as Secure.

Most people don't change their attachment styles, but it is entirely possible to do so. Any individual with one of the less-healthy styles can develop more secure qualities with tremendous self-work. In order for this to happen, however, the individual must pursue therapy and/or seek out the companionship of someone with a secure attachment style. By cultivating self-awareness and a willingness to develop better habits, anyone can transition out of their unhealthy behavior.

Must-Know Tips for Starting a New Relationship When You Have a History of Bad Relationships

Do you have one of the first three attachment styles? If so, you've probably had a few bad relationships, maybe even abusive relationships. You may be working through some negative or even outright destructive behavior, but rest assured, it is possible to move on. Plenty of people have done it on their own. And with a loving companion by your side, you can work on it together.

The trauma we endure can shape the way we communicate with our partners and the imagined stressors we're more likely to experience. For this reason, we may express more fear, anger, or distress in situations that would not normally upset someone. This isn't always fair on our partners, especially since they aren't the ones that hurt us, and it's important we don't become abusive ourselves or cause our new partners pain. Keep the following tips in mind to maintain your emotional and mental health, while also being considerate of your partner.

Please note that if your trauma is severe, these tips are not meant to substitute for help from a mental health professional.

1. Make a list of behavior you will no longer tolerate

In order to turn over a new leaf successfully, it's essential that we identify what we wish to remove from our lives. If you've had a history of experiencing pain, make a list of behavior in previous partners that caused you significant pain. This list is exactly what you should no longer tolerate in relationships from now on. There's no way to make excuses for future abusive partners because this list makes it simple; they either did it or they didn't. Refer back to it to remind yourself of its contents and feel free to show it to new partners once you're seriously dating.

Having this list is also helpful because during times of emotional distress, our feelings can cloud our judgment. It can save us from directing unwarranted anger or upset at partners who didn't do anything wrong. For example, if you're having a bad day, you may feel more suspicious or anxious than usual. If your partner does something, you may overreact. Looking back at your list, you'll see that your partner didn't actually exhibit the behavior you outlined. This will make it clear that the feeling likely comes from within, because you're having a bad day.

For this list to be truly successful, we should strictly write down behavior and not emotions. Adding to your list that you will not tolerate anyone causing you pain makes things tricky; sometimes we can impose pain on ourselves and mistakenly believe it is the fault of our partners. And feel free to get an outside opinion on whether the behavior noted down is sufficient and reasonable.

2. When you're ready, share what happened with your new partner

In order for our partners to support us in the best way possible, they need to know what they're dealing with. Without knowledge of what happened and how it affected us, they'll have no clue how to help. Share with them what happened, what you need from them, and what you're doing to help yourself move on.

If you're not ready to tell them just yet, then wait till you're ready, but in the meantime, don't expect them to just *know* how to help. If you don't think you'll be ready to share with them any time soon, feel free to ask a friend to tell your new partner. Although this isn't the ideal way of letting them know, it is better than leaving them in the dark. All in all, it's always best for your new partner to have as much information as possible so they can offer the exact support you need.

3. Rely on your support system whenever necessary

Our closest friends and family are our greatest allies. If you're ever unsure, use them as your sounding board and ask them for an outside opinion. Our feelings are not always trustworthy since past trauma makes us more predisposed to feel a certain way. Ask someone you trust who can give you a neutral opinion. Don't make all the big decisions on your own.

Furthermore, it's also essential that the person you're relying on for advice is someone whose love life you seek to emulate. Opinions are not all made equal. If a person in a healthy relationship gives you one piece of advice, but ten people in bad relationships say the opposite, you should always listen to the person who has lived the outcome you most desire. Look for the most neutral people possible; if you struggle with jealousy, don't get advice from someone who also struggles with jealousy.

4. Resist making comparisons to previous partners

When we're in a new relationship, it is completely natural for our brains to use past relationships and partners as reference points. This is just what the brain does to try and understand a new situation. Although the instinct is natural, keep in mind that its analyses are not always correct. When we encounter new territory, our past experiences are a highly limited pool of knowledge to extrapolate from.

Make the effort to remind yourself that your current partner is not your previous partner. Your brain will try to make comparisons, but resist them when you can. If the attitude your new partner exhibits is different to what you previously experienced, then remind yourself there's no reason to expect the same outcome. If there's no real evidence, there's no reason to believe the worst. If your previous partner cheated on you with a friend of the opposite sex, remember that there are many individuals who don't do this. There's no reason to become angry or upset right off-the-bat. Your current partner did not hurt you like your previous partner, so do not punish them for something they didn't do.

It is especially important that we don't vocalize any comparisons to previous partners. If our current partner did nothing wrong, this will come across as very insulting. If you get the urge to do this in the heat of the moment, resist it at all costs.

5. Do not expect your partner to fix everything for you

You should definitely expect support from your partner during times of healing. However, there's a big difference between support and an emotional or psychological crutch. Support crosses the line into 'crutch' territory when you stop doing things for yourself. Instead of doing the self-work to transform your behavior and thinking patterns, you expect your partner to change *their* behavior. There is suddenly intense pressure on the 'crutch' partner to fix everything and if anything goes wrong, it automatically becomes their fault. Avoid this dynamic at all costs! This is a sure way to get your partner to resent you and no one would blame them – forcing someone to be your crutch is cruel!

When we engage in dynamics like this, we immediately become stagnant. Since someone else is babying us, we are never challenged, and this means we won't grow. Remember that feeling uncomfortable isn't always bad. We should always examine our discomforts and see if it's something we can work on, before asking someone to change. Don't expect your partner to meet all your needs (and more!) without meeting any of theirs in return. A history of bad relationships is not a good excuse to take advantage of a new partner.

6. Start making self-care an essential part of your routine

One powerful thing we can do for ourselves is engage in self-care practices. Ditch the idea that self-care is only for special occasions and incorporate it into your daily or weekly routine. Self-care does not have to cost any money; it just means you're allowing yourself to do whatever it is that makes you feel calm and taken care of. You know it's self-care when you reconnect to who you are and when you feel at peace. This can mean taking a warm bubble bath and listening to your favorite music. Or this can mean going to a relaxing cafe, journaling, and reading a great book or treating yourself to some baked goods. If you've got a bigger budget, you can get a massage and indulge in chocolate. The possibilities are endless!

When we start making self-care part of our routine, we also rewire our brain to feel its effects more often. It's not just the bubble bath or massage that becomes the new norm, the peace and calm becomes more of a norm as well. This is essential when we're recovering from trauma because we are in deep need of rewiring responses and impulses. In addition to this, however, it is a powerful symbol for the new chapter you will begin. By carving out time to focus on you, you are vowing to start thinking of your needs more often. You are recognizing your importance and you are saying no to relationships that cause you pain. Self-care for the win.

Chapter Seven - The Ticking Time Bomb

When we're considering potential partners, we tend to put too much weight in excitement and passion. While that's, no doubt, extremely important, we neglect what really makes the meat of a relationship. Almost anyone can bring a fun time to the table, but what will they do during the hard times? The dark nights when an argument goes round in circles? When voices are raised and it feels like your blood is boiling? The way you and your partner behave and react in these situations has the biggest bearing on your relationship. Your sex life and the number of interests you have in common: neither of these factors are a true test of your strength as a team. The biggest signifier of your relationship's strength is how you fight and how you find solutions to problems.

Even if you're soulmates and you have a blast together every single day, there are going to be days and nights where you can't stand each other. While no one is perfect at the beginning of a relationship, it is essential that we learn over time. There will come a time when we need to handle a ticking time bomb (a highly sensitive situation) and in order to prevent it from exploding, the necessary knowledge and tools are required. Expect that challenges will arise and be prepared to solve them.

When to Press the Pause or Stop Button

Open communication can solve many problems, but there are times when you need to take a step back. Talking doesn't always make things better, sometimes it can cause damage and needless distress. If it's an important discussion, then press the pause button and resume the talk when both parties are more level-headed. If the conversation isn't about anything important, press stop and drop the topic like a hot potato. These are the signs you need to cool off and let it sit:

- **Emotions are running high**

If there are tears, raised voices, and you get the distinct feeling someone (and this includes you) might explode, press that pause button. When emotions get too charged and intense, there's a higher likelihood of someone boiling over and saying something hurtful. You may even make a decision you can't take back. To press pause successfully, say something like:

"I sense we're both getting too consumed by our emotions. Why don't we settle down and resume this conversation later? I want to solve this problem and in our current state, I don't think we can."

Once both parties have had a chance to cool off, you'll come back more rational and level-headed. A potential disaster will have been averted and you'll feel grateful for taking that break.

- **You've had this conversation before and it didn't end well**

For many couples, there can be recurring discussions that never seem to get solved. Some of these can bring out the worst in both partners and end in bitter, hurtful remarks that do a lot of damage. If you find this dead-end discussion cropping up again, nip it in the bud while you can. Consider saying:

"The last time we had this talk, we both said a lot of things we didn't mean. I feel that it did more harm than good, and I really don't want to see that situation repeated. I really want to fix this situation so how about we take some time to think about solutions? We can each think of ways to move forward. And we can resume this discussion when we have new ideas to bring to the table."

If the discussion has no bearing on the relationship, simply point out what happened last time, and say you feel it's best to agree to disagree. Each couple will have their own versions of dead-end topics, and you need to learn when it's not important to win.

- **At least one partner is tired**

When we're tired, we can sometimes lose the energy required to regulate ourselves and our emotions. That's not to say the emotions we feel when we are tired aren't real. In fact, oftentimes this can display what we really feel – but we become less able to deal with them maturely and effectively. When we have energy, our brain can easily go through the process of organizing our words and thoughts in a clear, constructive manner. When we don't have energy, our brains can fail to get this process started or do it properly.

When we enter an argument in this tired state, we are not using the best tools we have. We are not equipped to be in the arena and it's best we get out before we cause damage. In this state of mind, we are much more likely to overreact and say something we don't mean. We shouldn't always expect our partners to understand that we're just tired and move on. If what we say is genuinely hurtful, it can cause deep hurt. Do not get into serious talks with your partner when one partner cannot communicate effectively in that moment.

- **Words have started to get hurtful**

For one reason or another, a conversation can really start to sour. You'll know this is starting to happen because either your partner will say something that stings or you'll say something you normally wouldn't say. If you notice that tone and language are starting to get aggressive or mean, then you need to walk away immediately and cool off. This is the point in our arguments that we should always try to avoid. Our heated conversations should never hurt. And if it does, know that it has gone too far.

Don't just walk out without saying a word, as this will appear as storming off, which could only further anger your partner. Instead, point out to your partner that you've started to say things you don't mean, and emphasize that you don't want to co-create a situation that does lasting damage. Suggest that you both take time to calm down and think about more constructive ways of getting your points across.

- **The conversation is going around in circles**

This often happens when both partners are tired, especially when they've exhausted themselves by having such a drawn-out argument. You'll notice that the same points continue to be raised, the same responses made each time, and yet somehow you keep coming back to the same thing over and over.

This is a sign your conversation has gone around in circles. If someone doesn't end it soon, it will only continue to go on and on, and a solution will likely never be found. Try to point out the conversation has become circuitous as soon as you notice. It could end with hurtful statements made, but even if it doesn't, it's a huge waste of time and energy for both partners.

If you find a certain topic leads you around in circles a lot, consider having this conversation via email. When discussions are written out, it's much easier to see where the confusion lies. By examining the responses closely, it becomes clear why the discussion always becomes circuitous.

- **The outcome of the discussion won't actually affect the relationship**

If the conversation is getting heated, consider whether the topic actually matters. Let's say you've both started to argue about a topic on the news. Ask yourself what difference it makes if you both agree or disagree. Does disagreeing on this topic make you have less fun together? Does it hurt you in any way? Does it affect either of your abilities to be good partners for one another? If the answer is 'no' to all of these questions, then this topic is not that important. The outcome does not affect your relationship in any way – so don't rile yourselves up over nothing.

How to Bring Up Your Concerns the Right Way

If you're going to be in a happy, healthy relationship, you need to know how to raise your concerns the right way. In other words, without causing significant damage to your partner and while being honest enough to incite change. These are incredibly sensitive situations, so pay close attention to the following tips:

- **Choose timing carefully**

Remember what we said about paying attention to timing? That's even more important when we're about to have a big talk. Don't bring up serious conversations when your partner is having a bad day or when they are exhausted. This will not lead to a favorable outcome! You're best bet is always to approach your partner when they are rested, calm, and not going through a difficult time.

- **Resist saying "but…" to soften the blow**

We always think we're doing someone a favor by starting with a positive before getting to the negative – but this is actually not true. Take, for example, the statement: "I love how passionate you've become about home-decorating and I think you've got some great ideas, but I'm just not sure I like these new changes."

As soon as the "but" comes into play, the earlier part of the sentence doesn't mean anything. It can be even more upsetting because you've gotten your partner's hopes up by starting with something so positive, but these hopes are completely trampled on by the time you finish the sentence. Your partner is smart! They know the real point is everything that comes after the "but." Don't try to soften the blow with this (bad) technique, and instead do it through careful language. Speaking of which…

- **Utilize all you've learned about gentle and constructive language**

We brought up constructive language in an earlier chapter, and it's time to put that lesson to good use. This is the perfect time to use your "I" or "I feel" statements! Instead of voicing your concerns in terms of what your partner did, reframe them so it's about what you feel. Steer clear of absolute language and assumptions, and ensure no sentence starts with "you."

If you're upset about how they rarely help with chores, resist the urge to say, "You never help with chores and you don't care about how it affects me." Instead, try saying something like, "I feel like I'm not getting enough help with chores. I'd feel a lot better if we could have a more even distribution of tasks." Notice that there is no mention of "you" at all. This is ideal because your partner doesn't feel cornered and it doesn't make any assumptions. We are also reducing the chance of an argument because it's difficult to argue with how someone feels. That's their reality.

- **Prepare for pushback or questions**

You should always prepare for the possibility of your partner pushing back a little. This doesn't necessarily mean it'll be with anger or frustration, but if you think there's a chance it might happen, then definitely prepare for it. Consider all the ways your partner might try to argue with it and think of a constructive, confident answer. This is especially important if you're the more submissive partner and you have a tendency to give in. For example, the second partner in the previous scenario might say, "But I washed the dishes last week" or "But I'm not as good at doing chores as you." You know your partner well enough to anticipate with some accuracy what their protests might be. Even if their responses are infuriating, stay calm and constructive.

- **Conclude with solutions and positivity**

Don't just sit and stew in the problem at hand, be ready to come up with a solution. Your partner may have some ideas as well, but for the best outcome, bring your own ideas to the table. Think of the next step and give your partner a place to start. This is the best way to work through a concern because you're essentially saying "This problem is easy to solve and here, this is the perfect opportunity. We can start making things better right now!"

Going back to our example problem, the concerned partner could then say, "I think a great way to resolve this would be to take turns each week doing the chores. How about I do the rest of this week and you can start on Monday?" Notice how this makes the situation instantly seem more positive. The problem is not the point anymore, it's the solution.

As we mentioned in a previous point, it's not a good idea to start the discussion with a "but" statement where you go from positive to negative – but the reverse is a much better idea. Add the positive statement to the end of the conversation so it can end on a good note.

5 Statements to Instantly Defuse a Heated Discussion

It happens in every relationship. Sometimes you find yourself in a talk with your partner that's gone from perfectly chill to blazing hot – and not in a good way. Perhaps it's because they've just had a hard day and they're in a bad mood, or perhaps they just woke up on the wrong side of the bed. Whatever it is, you can't seem to tame the fire in their attitude and all you know is it needs to stop now. Keep these statements in your back pocket to immediately calm a heated situation:

1. "I see your point."

When we say this, we validate our partner's point of view. This can calm someone down because all we really want is to make our point understood. We continue arguing because we want to make ourselves heard. Eliminate the need to continue arguing, by saying they have already made themselves heard.

2. "I understand."

This statement is ideal for defusing a situation without giving in. By saying you understand you are not admitting you are wrong; you are just saying you comprehend their view. Similar to the previous statement, you are letting them know what they've said has been thoughtfully received.

3. "What can I do to make it better?"

Instead of fueling the argument, try shifting the conversation to possible solutions. Without stirring the pot, you're letting your partner know you're ready to fix the situation. This will make them more willing to cooperate. This statement works wonders, but you must be willing to put in extra work. Since you are letting your partner know you want to make things better, you need to follow up on that promise.

4. "What do you need right now?"

Like the previous response, you're skipping the argument and going straight to the solution. Your partner will be more touched by this question because you're asking them directly what they need. This can cut to the core of an argument because you're saying, "I know it's not really about this. I know it's about you, and what you're not getting. I want to take care of that." Take on a more nurturing attitude and be willing to do what your partner says they need.

5. "I'm sorry."

Don't underestimate the power of apologies. It can whittle a fiery blaze down to a single burning ember. Sometimes, it's just not worth arguing till our heads turn blue. Apologizing is not always about admitting defeat or letting your partner win, it's about choosing harmony over your ego. It doesn't always mean "You're right, I'm wrong" sometimes it can mean "It hurts me to see you so upset and I'm sorry you feel this way."

What NOT to Say During an Argument

We've covered what you should say. Now, let's get to what you definitely shouldn't say. If you're in a heated discussion or an argument, steer clear of the following phrases and sentences if you want to prevent an explosion.

1. "Calm down."

It's a big claim, but I'll say it: never in the history of mankind has an urge to "calm down" actually calmed an upset person down. Even if you mean well, this comes off as condescending and unsympathetic. The person who needs to calm down is actually in deep need of empathy and understanding; this statement demonstrates the opposite of that. It shows that the non-upset person doesn't understand at all, since they think it should be so easy for their partner to stop expressing their emotions in that moment. If you say this, you will not get a positive response. Avoid it at all costs and instead try asking them to share more with you.

2. "Not this again!"

If your partner is upset and you bemoan the fact they're upset about something *again,* this will only create more anger. By saying this, we're invalidating our partner. We're showing annoyance and impatience at their true feelings. We're essentially saying we don't care because they've been upset about it before. Instead of showing care, we are being condescending and implying their reaction is ridiculous.

3. "If you don't ____ then I'm breaking up with you."

This is a big no-no in relationships. In fact, many people consider it emotional abuse. If you're threatening your partner with a break-up in order to get them to do something, you're displaying cruel behavior, especially if you're not really serious. Even if you are, however, phrasing it as a threat could still cause a lot of damage. If your partner stops whatever they're doing and you continue to be in a relationship, this moment will leave them with a lot of anxiety. They will begin to feel as if they're walking on eggshells. If they start to make changes for you, they will only be acting out of fear, instead of love.

To properly convey how you feel without resorting to threats, remember to use "I" statements. Instead of saying, "If you don't stop talking to him, I'm breaking up with you" try saying, "I feel very upset by how much you talk to this other guy. It's starting to bother me on a deep level and I worry it's affecting my ability to be a healthy partner for you."

9 Relationship Problems You Cannot Fix

Try as hard as you may, there are some issues in a relationship that cannot be helped nine out of ten times. You may be a master communicator, and perhaps even your partner as well, but sometimes, there's only so much you can do. If your relationship has any of the following problems, it may be best to walk away before both partners begin to hurt.

1. Serial cheating

One instance of infidelity can really tear a relationship to shreds, but even then, it's salvageable – if the cheating partner makes lasting changes to their behavior. But continuous infidelity is a different issue. This indicates the cheating partner has a real problem, and they can't be in a healthy relationship until they solve it on their own. Stop making allowances for a partner that constantly cheats on you. It will only lead to more pain. No amount of good communication will fix this. It is entirely up to the cheating partner to do the self-work. And if they haven't started now, why wait around and continue to get hurt?

2. Too much contempt

It's normal to be mad at your partner for something, but contempt is a different story. Contempt runs deeper and is far more persistent. It happens when one partner can't let something go. It's begun to gnaw at them, they can't forget it or forgive, and it's caused resentment to build. The fault could be anyone's. It could be the non-contemptuous partner's fault for deeply hurting his or her partner, or it could be the contemptuous partner's fault for refusing to heal and let go. A little scorn is normal after an upsetting event, but it transforms into contempt when time has passed, and time has healed no wounds whatsoever.

3. Narcissistic personality disorder

There's a big difference between being a narcissist and being a clinical Narcissist, i.e. having Narcissistic Personality Disorder. If your partner is a little vain, occasionally makes big-headed statements, but can still take accountability for his mistakes, then your partner is likely just a regular lowercase narcissist. They may be annoying sometimes, but they don't have a personality disorder, and you can still make progress with them. A Narcissist, on the other hand, cannot be fixed and it's best to step away now before you get more hurt. Clinical Narcissists are unable to take accountability for anything and they have an unwillingness to recognize the needs of other people. It is not possible for them to be in a healthy, happy relationship.

4. Conflicting goals

You may have all the same common interests, but at the end of the day, conflicting goals can be a killer. Some partners may be lucky enough to settle on a compromise, but some goals are on opposite ends of the spectrum. If you desperately want kids and your partner doesn't want them at all, there's no way to compromise on this. Unless someone changes their mind, both partners cannot get what they want and this means one partner is doomed to feel unsatisfied. This can lead to resentment and may even ruin a connection. In the end, it can result not only in pain, but a lot of wasted time.

5. Abuse

If one partner engages in abusive behavior, whether physical or emotional, the relationship should end as soon as possible. Abusive behavior is toxic and will only drag both partners into a cycle of pain that continues on until it's off-the-charts. The abusive partner is always at fault and their behavior demonstrates they are incapable of being in a healthy relationship at the current stage in their life. It is advised that this partner leaves the relationship, stops hurting the other partner, and pursues therapy so they evolve into more healthy, loving companion.

The abusive partner is less likely to admit what they're doing is a problem, so it may be up to the abused partner to find the strength to leave. Friends and family are in the best position to end such a volatile relationship. If you are close to someone who is suffering from abuse, see if you can assist in getting them out of the bad situation.

6. Failure to grow

Conflict is a natural part of any relationship, and if both partners are healthy, they should be finding ways to achieve better harmony. For one reason or another, however, one or both partners may find there's a persistent lack of growth. In other words, there's a quality or behavior pattern that has continued to have a negative effect without any improvement, even though our partner knows we want to see change. This is only a big problem if the behavior that needs to be grown out of is affecting the happiness of the relationship.

For example, if your partner has been working on his anger issues for years but is still as turbulent as he was in the beginning, reconsider whether you can put up with this for the future to come. If your partner continues to flirt with other people even though you've repeatedly pointed out it bothers you, it's likely this will not ever change. At a certain point, it becomes clear when certain issues are here to stay and it's important that we make the right decision concerning our future. Either this behavior is too deeply ingrained in their personalities or they aren't motivated to seek out this growth. Choose what's right for your sanity and stop waiting for change that likely won't come.

7. Constant and pointless arguing

We may go through periods of bickering with our partners – especially if we're going through a rough patch in our lives – but if this occurrence is persistent and a constant drain on your energy, it's time to stop and think. Frequent pointless arguing is often a sign of a much deeper problem. Sometimes both partners have stopped being compatible, fallen out of love, or have developed deep resentment for each other. It's very rare that these problems can be fixed. If it has become easier to be apart from your partner than be with them, it may be time to put a cork in it.

8. Inability to trust

It's true what they say; without trust, a relationship is nothing. Trust forms the foundation of every relationship. And without a strong foundation, it doesn't matter how glamorous and impressive the rest of it is, it'll come crumbling down as soon as the wind changes. Once trust is broken, it's extremely difficult to rebuild. It can take years and a lot of hard work if a couple decides to try and make it work, and even then, sometimes it is not successful. In every relationship, we should have the basic assurance that our partner won't hurt or betray us. Consider how deeply broken the trust is and whether you ever see yourself fully recovering.

9. Deep feelings for a third party

We can all get over lust or a mild crush, but if it's more than that, we're dealing with something else entirely. Sometimes, the feelings one partner has for a third party are very deep, and they may even be verging on love. For feelings to get to this point, the partner in question would have to be exposed to this third party for an extended period of time. We know this because it takes a while for deep feelings to develop.

There's a lot less hope for the relationship if the partner in question has been intentionally seeking out the company of this third party. This behavior displays a big problem with self-control – and this could pose a serious problem to the relationship down the road. If this scenario takes place, it may be beneficial for the relationship to end.

It's a slightly different story if the partner with feelings has developed them due to involuntary exposure, for example, through work. In this case, it is not a self-control issue and there is hope. The only way to fix it, however, is by completely removing oneself from all situations involving the third party. If this is a co-worker, it means making a big decision, such as quitting the job causing exposure. Otherwise, these feelings will only grow.

The good news is that the majority of partners can, indeed, work through their problems. If your relationship issue wasn't listed, there are higher chances for you working out your issues. And while the problems listed are mostly unfixable, there will always be exceptions. In any case, it always takes a lot of hard work, kind communication, and incredible cooperation to see positive change.

Chapter Eight - Deepening the Bond

A short message from the Author:

Hey! We've made it to the final chapter of the audiobook and I hope you've enjoyed it so far.

If you have not done so yet, I would be incredibly thankful if you could take just a minute to leave a quick review on Audible, even if it's just a sentence or two!

Many readers and listeners don't know how hard reviews are to come by, and how much they help an author.

To do so, just click the 3 dots in the top right corner of your screen inside of your Audible app and hit the "Rate and Review" button.

Then you'll be taken to the "rate and review" page where you can enter your star rating and then write a sentence or two.

It's that simple!

I look forward to reading your review as I personally read every single one.

I am very appreciative as your review truly makes a difference for me.

Now back to your scheduled programming.

There's always more we can do to deepen the bond in our relationship. At the end of the day, we shouldn't just feel like lovers; we should also feel like friends and to an extent, family. When we feel a strong connection to our partners, there is a much higher likelihood that communication will be kind, helpful, and transformative. And in addition to this, a good connection means we're much more likely to follow up on our compromises and be a better partner. When we feel close to someone, we instantly feel more compassionate and empathetic. These two qualities are necessary for a loving connection.

As excellent as these bonding techniques may be, they require commitment from both partners to be completely effective. A positive outcome takes effort and attention; it does not simply fall into your lap after one attempt. Keep these activities and exercises in mind for the rest of your future to come. Even when relationship communication is good, this is no reason to stop seeking out opportunities to bond.

Exercises and Activities that Strengthen Relationships

- **Start a love journal with your partner**

This practice does wonders for maintaining romantic connections. Start off by purchasing a journal (ideally together) that you both love the look of. If you don't live together, then aim to take turns with the journal. Come up with a schedule that works for you. Will the journal pass hands weekly? Fortnightly? Whenever you feel like it? Whatever works for you!

If you do live together, keep the journal in a private area of the house, but one where you frequently pass by. Again, the arrangement of who and when to write is up to you. I advise writing something every day, even if it's very short, or taking turns. If you decide to take turns, find a creative way to indicate who the last writer was, without opening the book. This will ensure you aren't constantly checking it to see if it's been updated.

What's great about this activity is that you can make the rules. Will the book be filled with love letters? Will it all be written in haikus? If one partner is upset, should they write an honest, open letter about how they feel in the journal? Or will this only be reserved for romance? It's totally up to you.

- **Role reversal**

This exercise is great for when two people are trying to see eye-to-eye on a problem. For this exercise to succeed, you and your partner should both be calm and willing to fully cooperate. If there's a hint of snark or sarcasm, abandon the attempt and try again during a better mood.

In this role reversal exercise, you and your partner will have a conversation about a problem at hand, but you'll both speak from the other person's point-of-view. Each of you should really think about what the other partner would say and consider real reasons they might use. One of the reasons this exercise is so effective is because it eliminates the need to "win" the discussion. Partners are forced to think deeply about their loved one's perspective, and this instantly helps couples empathize with each other.

- **The eye contact exercise**

For this exercise, you and your partner should sit across from each other. Ideally, lights should be dim and you should be close to each other, but not too close. Wherever you choose to sit, make sure it's comfortable. It's also important there's no talking or touching during this exercise.

Set a timer for five minutes and aim to look into each others' eyes for the full length of those five minutes. Eye contact should be gentle and uninterrupted. Do not stare intensely at your partner and always remember to blink as you would normally.

You might be surprised by how fast five minutes goes by. Couples can get so lost that they actually lose track of time. After this exercise, you'll feel a heightened sense of connection and attunement with your partner. If a distance has grown between the two of you, this exercise can help bring you back to the same wavelength.

- **Create a vision board**

Get creative with your partner and work on a vision board together. A vision board is a motivational collage of photos, notes, and anything that gets across the future you'd most like to have together. This can include places you'd like to travel to or photos of your dream house together. Whatever fills you both with hope, joy, and positivity about what's to come. It's important that both partners contribute something to this vision board. Remember that it's your *shared* vision, not just one partner's fantasy. And most of all, have fun with it. This is an incredibly fun way to strengthen your connection with your partner. You don't need an artistic streak to enjoy it!

- **Go through the famous '36 Questions that Lead to Love'**

In a famous experiment conducted by psychologists, a significant number of people felt a stronger connection after going through a series of questions together. Many of them even claimed to have fallen in love. Ultimately, the experiment proves that when both partners are engaging in personal self-disclosure, acting vulnerably, and actively listening to their partner, an immediate connection is formed. By forcing two people to do just this, a sense of closeness and intimacy was fostered. Although this experiment was conducted on people who didn't know each other, existing couples still benefit greatly from this bonding exercise.

The 36 questions are separated into three sets, which each one becoming more personal than the last. Take turns answering these questions:

<u>Set 1</u>

1. Whom would you invite to be your dinner guest, given the choice of absolutely anyone in the world?

2. Would you like to be famous? If so, in what way?

3. Before making a phone call, do you rehearse what you're going to say? If so, why do you do this?

4. What constitutes a perfect day in your eyes?

5. When was the last time you sang to yourself? And when was the last time you sang for someone else?

6. If you lived to the age of 90 and had the choice of either the body or mind of a 30-year old for the last 60-years of your life, which would you choose?

7. Do you have any idea how you might die?

8. List three things that you and your partner seem to have in common.

9. What are you most grateful for about your life?

10. If you could change anything at all about the way you were raised, what would you change?

11. Share your life story in as much detail as possible but take only 4 minutes and no longer.

12. If you could acquire any quality or ability overnight, what would you choose?

Set 2

13. If you came upon a crystal ball that could tell you any truth about your life, yourself, your future, or anything else, what would you most want to know?

14. Is there anything that you've dreamed of doing for a long time but haven't ever done? Why haven't you done it yet?

15. What would you say is the greatest accomplishment of your life?

16. What are the qualities and behaviors you most value in a friendship?

17. Talk about your most treasured memory.

18. Now talk about your worst memory.

19. If you knew that you'd die suddenly in a year, is there anything you'd change about the way you're living now? What would that be and why?

20. Describe what friendship means to you.

21. How important are love and affection to you? What roles do they play in your life?

22. Take turns sharing a positive characteristic about each other. Each partner should share five things for a total of ten.

23. How close is your family? Are you warm towards each other? Do you think your childhood was happier than the average childhood?

24. What's your relationship with your mother like? How do you feel about it?

Set 3

25. Take turns sharing three statements, each one beginning with "we." For example, "we're in this room feeling…"

26. Finish this sentence: "I wish I had someone with whom I could share…"

27. If you and your partner were to become close friends, what would be important for them to know?

28. Tell your partner what you honestly like them. This time, try and share something you wouldn't normally say to someone you'd just met.

29. Talk about one of the most embarrassing moments of your life.

30. When was the last time you cried in front of another person? When was the last time you cried by yourself?

31. Share something that you like about your partner already.

32. In your opinion, what is too serious to be joked about, if anything?

33. If you were to die tonight without the opportunity to communicate with anyone, what would you most regret not having told someone? Why haven't you told them yet?

34. Your house, containing everything you own, catches fire. You've saved your loved ones and pets, and now you only have time to save one more item. What would you save? Why?

35. Of all the people in your family, whose death upset and disturb you the most? Why?

36. Share a personal problem with your partner and ask for their advice on how they might handle it. After this, the partner who offered advice should reflect how the asker seems to be feeling about the chosen problem.

Bond Instantly with these 8 Fun Couple Activities

When it comes down to it, the secret to nurturing your bond is stepping outside of your comfort zone and giving your partner your full attention. Feel free to seek that out in any way you choose, but I highly advise starting with these highly effective methods well known for strengthening bonds instantly.

1. Massaging each other

This highly sensual act does more than heat things up, it also asks each partner to engage in a few moments of total kindness towards their loved one. For the length of each massage, one partner is giving completely to their partner without getting anything in return. They are focused on their partner's pleasure entirely and concerned only with creating an enjoyable experience for them through the power of touch. People are so accustomed to physical intimacy and touch strictly being part of sex that it can be wildly exciting to have both those things without sexual contact. This closeness through non-sexual touch is what creates the bond. For the best outcome, both partners should take turns and each massage should take the same length of time.

2. Go out dancing

Dancing is about as close as you can get to sexual intercourse without actually having it! For that reason, dancing can be a real fire-starter in a relationship; not just in the passion department, but even in terms of our connection. It doesn't matter what language you speak or what culture you're from, dancing has a knack for inducing joy and releasing tension in the body. When we do this with our partner, we're expressing ourselves without saying a word. The act of moving in alignment and in rhythm with each other is its own collaborative exercise, and it can be a wonderful symbol for loving each other in harmony. If you and your partner are on the shier side, why not have a drink or two to open you up?

3. Work out together

Believe it or not, numerous studies have proven that working out with your partner boosts overall happiness in your relationship. Researchers have found that this is particularly true for exercises that require both partners to get up and move together in some fashion. Bonding happens at a subconscious level when we engage in the mirror effect. This is the neurological process that leads to bonding and manifests as mirrored movements. By coordinating our actions or mirroring each other's movements, we are firing off mirror neurons and subsequently, deepening our bond.

And that's not all! Studies have also found that working out with a partner leads to improved workout performances. When someone is watching, we are more likely to push harder to try and avoid looking weak. Bond harder and get hotter: doesn't that sound like a great idea?

4. Go on a fancy date

The reason fancy dates have such a positive effect is simple: it gets us out of our routine and forces us to make ourselves look good for our partner. It's no secret that when we take care of ourselves and our appearance, our partner will find us more attractive. Couple this with an exciting scenario you don't normally experience and *voila,* you've started to reboot your connection. If your relationship has started to feel too comfortable, then consider taking your partner out to a nice restaurant. The formality of a fancy date offers a refreshing change from lounging around in sweatpants and it can instantly spice up a boring relationship.

5. Visit the location of one of your "firsts"

Every couple has a unique love story. Even if it wasn't love at first sight or you had an unconventional start, it can be nice to take a walk down memory lane every once in a while. Why not visit the place where you met or where you had your first kiss? Retracing our steps can remind us of how far we've come with our significant other. If you do this with your partner, you'll relive the rush and the butterflies for just a moment; places attached to strong memories inevitably send us back in time. Enjoy these memories with each other and savor the beauty of your one-of-a-kind story, even if it wasn't perfect. Remember that at one point in time, where you are now was where you hoped to be.

6. Go on a trip together

A study conducted by the U.S. Travel Association found that couples who travel together are a great deal more satisfied in their relationships than those who don't. Still, many couples are hesitant to go on a trip because they're convinced that doing this will drain their bank account. This isn't true at all.

To experience the benefits of travel, all couples need to do is to get out of their comfort zone (not just psychologically but geographically as well!) and see something new and exciting. If you've got the budget for it, then sure, visit Paris or Rome, but you can have just as much fun going on a road trip to the next state over. Visit a National Park and stay at a 2 or 3-star hotel, or a humble inn. Get out into nature. Do something you don't normally do. This change of scenery can provide a much needed break from your rigid routine and you'll find your bond deepening naturally as you experience the wider world together.

7. Visit an amusement park

Kid or not, let's face it, amusement parks are incredibly fun. If you don't have a crippling fear of heights, take a break from your routine and spend a day at one with your significant other. Your relationship will see a number of benefits. For starters, thrilling rides will give you a rush of endorphins, meaning you'll feel overcome with happy feelings and a natural high. You'll also be pumped through with adrenaline, a neurotransmitter which is known to create memories in the mind. This means the wonderful day you've had will be solidified in your mind as a happy memory. Since you and your partner are encountering anxiety-inducing situations, you'll bond as you both seek out comfort and warmth in each other.

8. Cook together

If you're on a budget, cooking together is a great way to deepen the bond while also filling the belly. Cooking requires both partners to cooperate and work towards a common goal – exactly what being in a successful relationship is all about! This is great practice for getting in the right mindset for problem-solving and teamwork. Each partner is making their own contribution and the process challenges both partners to get on the same page, or the entire meal suffers.

A cooking project teaches us skills we need to bring into the rest of our relationship. And on top of this, we bond because we're creating something together. We're combining efforts for a tangible finished product. If we succeed in making a delicious meal, couples can bond over the shared pride. They'll likely feel like they can do anything as a team. But those who don't succeed, should not feel discouraged. This is not a reflection on your relationship; you may just need some more cooking practice!

Scroll through cooking websites or recipe books and decide on a meal that you'd like to recreate. This should be something you both love. If you're not experienced cooks, choose a dish with simple-enough instructions that you understand and make sure you possess all the necessary equipment.

Even the closest couples need to take time out to deepen their bond. It doesn't mean it's not already deep, it's about reaching out and reconnecting to remind yourselves why you're there. Time and routine can wear us down; seek out moments of intimacy to strengthen your bond. When we act from a place of deep bonding, relationship communication is more likely to be loving and effective.

Keep an open heart and be brave enough to leave your comfort zone so as to meet each other's need for adventure and variety. Instead of feeling mindless panic in an uncertain scenario, try and transform that feeling into the desire to problem-solve with your partner. Approach life with the mindset that you can do anything if you put your heads together, and you can solve any need you have, if you put your hearts together.

Conclusion

Congratulations on making it to the end of *Relationship Communication*! Whether you realize it or not, you've made one giant leap in the right direction. This isn't just fantastic for you, but for your significant other. You'll both see benefits that impact your day-to-day habits and with continued practice of these techniques, the days of strained communication will feel long gone. By completing this book, you've demonstrated your commitment to more effective and loving communication – and this is one of the best things you could possibly do for the person you love. You're on the right track towards a stronger relationship. You should be proud of yourself!

While you've made a big first step, it's essential that you don't quit now. Relationship communication is an ongoing journey; you've been granted the tools and techniques, but now it's time to use them in real situations, in the real world. Don't make this a short-lived attempt, but incorporate these transformative practices into your daily life and make them last. Reinvent your norms entirely and create exemplary habits.

Make sure you understand the five vital needs that your relationship must fulfill for both partners to be happy. Perhaps work with your partner on identifying which of your needs have been fully met and which ones still remain unmet. This is an essential step to make before finding a solution. Once you've done this, assess your situation and see if you can figure out which stage your relationship is in. This will help you better understand what you're going through, and equally as helpful, it'll show you what else is to come.

I sure hope you were honest with yourself in the second chapter. Don't feel ashamed to admit your relationship has a problem. After all, we *must* do this before we can start making positive changes. Hopefully, you identified the reason why communication has been less than great and you've finally been made aware of any mistakes you're currently making. But of course, don't just dwell on these problems. As I mentioned, you need to start creating better habits. You've learned all about the habits that save relationships. Start using these right away!

You've delved deeper into the many ways we can express and receive love. Once you've worked out what your partner's love language is, try and think of creative ways to show them how much you care. In fact, I highly recommend going over the section with them so you, too, can let your love language be known. When couples have a good understanding of each other's love languages, a lot less becomes lost in translation. Suddenly both partners are on the same page. Without all the confusion of trying to understand each other, they can just focus on the exchange of love.

While habits are certainly helpful, the two people at the core of the relationship must be healthy halves of the whole to really make it work. In order to form a great partnership and be a good partner, it's necessary that we learn to be emotionally healthy individuals. We don't become perfect once we enter into a relationship; all the emotional baggage and trauma we experienced beforehand comes with us! If we're not careful, past hurts can seep into our communication habits and tinge them with negativity. With the new tools you've been provided with, you can focus all your energy on becoming a better partner. You can finally start putting the past behind you. Try and help your partner do the same. At the end of the day, make sure you're meeting each others' needs – not just the five basic ones, but also the unique needs that come with their personalities.

Treat every sensitive situation with care. Know when you are dealing with a ticking time-bomb, and refer back to the relevant chapter for the techniques you need during the hard conversations. By following this guide closely, you'll ensure that even through the harsh storms, you always stay afloat. There is no such thing as completely smooth sailing in a relationship, but you can survive and make the most of the journey with these important tools. When we handle these situations the right way, they become opportunities for deeper intimacy. They become open doors instead of walls and dead-ends.

Relationship communication doesn't come naturally to anyone; it always takes work, commitment, and incredible self-discipline. It is a choice that loving partners make for each other everyday, and those that make the effort, reap rewards that others can scarcely imagine. Stay self-aware and do what you can to deepen your bond. Even people who are exceptionally close need to find time to maintain their connection. Let the love you foster through these lessons power every interaction from now on. I've shown you the wonderful path ahead, now it's your turn to walk it together.

NO MORE CODEPENDENCY

Healthy Detachment Strategies to Break the Pattern. *Discover How to Stop Struggling with Codependent Relationships, Obsessive Jealousy, and Narcissistic Abuse*

Table of Contents

Introduction

At first glance, codependent relationships look completely healthy. There appears to be trust, care, and closeness – and what could possibly be bad about that? Look a little closer and you'll see there's more than meets the eye. Both partners appear to have distinct roles and you'll notice they seem to be stuck in a cycle. One partner is the carer or the 'fixer' while the other partner receives an excessive degree of support which holds them back from any personal growth. Now that you see it up close, you recognize this unhealthy pattern for what it is; it's codependency.

If you're in a codependent relationship, you'll know this one-sided dynamic well. Perhaps you're the enabler, intent on helping your partner so much that you end up doing everything for them – even allowing their damaging habits to wreak havoc. Or perhaps you're the enabled partner, suffering from an ailment, addiction, or mental health condition, and you find yourself relying on your significant other a lot to help you get through each day. Until now, you've been taught to believe that your behavior is indicative of love, but I'm here to tell you that you are very wrong.

Codependency is a deeply dysfunctional condition. When it takes over a relationship, it can hold partners back from professional success, sever cords with family members and friends, cause deep emotional or psychological wounding, and in the long run, it'll create resentment in the relationship. This may result in the ruin of the partnership at hand, meaning everything they've lost along the way was all for nothing. As soon as codependency is identified, it must be stopped or this immense damage will be caused.

In this book, I'm going to help you put a stop to your codependent ways so you can finally be in the healthy, happy relationship you desire. I'll take you from clinging codependent partners to empowered individuals who are on top of their respective worlds. Even if you've been stuck in this destructive cycle for a long time, I'll show you how to quit it for good.

I am proud to say I'm a recovered codependent. Since I evolved out of my codependent habits several years ago, I've helped many codependent couples break out of their harmful relationship patterns. I know your struggles better than most people. I've been there and I understand the aching to be needed – and how it feels to not know who you are, when you aren't needed. I'm living proof that it gets better and that your relationship can feel a million times more fulfilling, loving, and empowering, if you just have the right tools and information. That's exactly what I'll be giving you. In this book, I'll be sharing all the insights that I learned on my journey from codependent to completely in power. Everything that I learned the hard way, I'll tell you simply so you don't have to make the same mistakes that I did. I'll show you how I transformed my unhealthy, troubling relationship into a powerful partnership that still thrives to this day – even twenty years down the road!

Your relationship is meant to thrive. Soon, you'll finally understand what that really means. You'll no longer feel desperate and exhausted by your partner. You'll know how to meet your partner's needs while also meeting your own. You'll know how to give your partner the absolute best, while also relishing certain rewards for yourself. For the first time, your relationship will have true balance and you'll experience what it's really like to love deeply, and be deeply loved in return.

I've worked with many couples that others deemed 'too far gone' and they've all seen a full recovery from their codependent ways. Those who once felt stuck, now know what it's like to evolve and grow. The truth is, breaking codependency doesn't just change your relationship, it transforms your entire life. People I've worked with continue to reap the benefits of their self-work to this day. The help I offered them is exactly what I'll be giving you in this book.

Codependent or not, let's not forget that we all want to find ourselves in loving relationships that bring joy to our lives. This is a commonality we all share. What makes you different is you've gotten caught up in the wrong habits and dysfunctional patterns. With my help, you'll finally remove these obstacles. You can enjoy all that is wonderful about your relationship, while leaving behind everything that frustrates and upsets you.

Here's the first tip I'll give you: start now! As time goes on, codependent couples become more fixed in their ways, finding it harder to break their harmful dynamic. Each moment you waste being codependent is a moment you waste not living up to your full potential. What are you and your partner missing out on while you cling to these destructive patterns? What wonderful experiences or accomplishments could be yours *right now* if you just made space for it to bloom?

By turning to the next page, you'll have made the first step to reclaiming your life from codependency. This is an exciting time – the end of a dark era and the rise of a new dawn where you'll finally be free from the shackles of codependency. Get ready for the new chapter of your life.

Chapter 1: Are You Codependent?

Codependency is an uncomfortable topic for many couples and this is partially due to a big misconception about what the term truly means. The word 'codependent' is thrown around a lot in the modern world, used to describe any couple that is extremely close or spends a lot of time together. These definitions are, of course, completely inaccurate. Codependency is many steps above infatuation or intimacy. It is far more than just reliance or dependence. True codependence does a huge disservice to both partners in a relationship, keeping them anchored in unhealthy habits that are slowly ruining their lives. It's about time we stopped using the term 'codependency' so lightly. Its effects can be brutal, if left unchecked.

In a healthy relationship, both partners give and take from each other in equal measure. You do this chore, I'll do that chore. You pay for dinner tonight, I'll cook dinner tomorrow. It may not always be as straightforward as this and there may be times when the exchange is slightly off-balance – for example, during times of stress, illness or trauma – but this in itself is not unhealthy. This in itself is not codependency. It's normal to see this fluctuation over time. Life happens and we're not always at the top of our game. During the low points, dependence on our partner or loved ones is completely natural. So, let's consider an important question: when exactly does reliance cross the line? When does dependence become codependence?

What it Means to Be Codependent

In a codependent relationship, two dysfunctional personalities find the ultimate enabler in each other. One partner desperately needs someone to take care of them and the other partner feels their self-worth is rooted in how much they are needed. These two personalities attract each other like magnets. Without self-awareness or a helpful third party, this can make a pretty toxic cocktail – one that's definitely not sustainable in the long-run. The needed partner takes on the role of 'giver' or 'rescuer' while the needy partner behaves like a troubled victim, 'taking' from the other partner and displaying an excessive need of care. The codependent giver responds to this need for care by overhelping or overextending their assistance.

This is different from everyday reliance in an ordinary relationship because codependency allows unhealthy behavior to continue. While it's completely normal to expect your partner to pick up the groceries sometimes or cook a meal when you're exhausted from work, it's not normal when one partner is consistently acting as the helper. At times, the giver may even take on a parental role, constantly making sure their partner is okay and helping them perform everyday activities they should be able to do themselves. The needy partner gets away with doing very little while the needed partner does nearly everything. Both dysfunctions fuel each other.

The term 'codependency' used to refer strictly to the toxic relationships of addicts and their partners, but today, it has expanded to include any relationship where self-destructive behaviors are allowed to continue. A codependency may enable any of the following behaviors:

- **Addiction** to substances such as drugs, alcohol, gambling, or any other compulsive activities causing financial strain and other damage to their personal life.
- **Poor mental health**, especially destructive symptoms brought about by personality disorders or depression.
- **Immaturity** and other forms of irresponsibility, where the enabler feels they have no choice but to accept this behavior because there's no way to change their partner and that's 'just how they are.'
- **Underachievement,** which may or may not be related to any of the above behaviors. The underachieving partner is not pulling

their weight financially or giving up on personal goals, and the enabler allows this to continue.

Codependency: So What?

Here's a question I hear a lot: "So what if a couple is codependent? If one partner feels fulfilled as the helper and they happen to find someone that needs to be helped, what's the problem? No one is being forced to do anything they don't want to do! Maybe they're happy this way."

A codependent couple can indeed appear happy, but this brittle happiness rests entirely on their denial. When a codependent partner overhelps their partner, they hold back their loved one from emotional and psychological growth. Destructive behavior is allowed to run rampant. The relationship starts to function like a crutch, where the fragile partner never learns how to take care of their own needs. They no longer feel the urgency to fix their own problems. Instead, they expect someone else to pick up the slack. When a person is treated like a child, they become disempowered and disconnected from their own inner strength. They are not given the opportunity to psychologically mature. This needy attitude affects far more than their romantic life; in fact, it's likely their professional life is suffering too. After all, bosses and coworkers are a lot less understanding than our loving partners!

And matters are just as bad for codependent enablers. They may appear to accomplish more than their partners, but they're also being held back from their full potential. Enablers feel their self-worth is rooted in how needed they are and their ability to help – this is an extremely unhealthy way to determine one's value. Those with this mentality have a hard time recognizing and vocalizing their own needs because they constantly think someone else's needs are more important. Can anyone be truly happy if their needs aren't being met? Many codependent couples stay together for the long-term, but by the end, enablers are often resentful and exhausted by the life they've lived serving someone else, with little care for their own self.

Dependence vs. Codependence

In a loving relationship, it is expected and completely healthy for both partners to depend on each other. This is what being in a relationship is all about! Unfortunately, many codependent couples who fail to see their dysfunctional ways think they're only engaging in healthy dependence. If you're not well-versed in the patterns of codependency, it can be difficult to tell between the two. To help you differentiate between dependence and codependence, let's compare the two types of behavior.

Example #1

Dependent: Partner A is going through a rough time and Partner B feels bad for them. In an attempt to cheer Partner A up, Partner B does something special with hopes it'll make a positive difference. B understands he can't change anything, but he wants to at least bring a smile to A's face.

Codependent: When Partner A starts going through a rough time, Partner B feels he needs to help A solve the problem. Partner B will do everything he can to make his partner feel better. When the attempts don't seem to be working, Partner B will start to feel worthless, like he can't do anything right. Unless he can ease Partner A's suffering, he feels extreme frustration with himself.

Example #2

Dependent: Partner B wants to spend a day in nature alone to destress after an exhausting work week. He tells Partner A his plan and she encourages him to do whatever he needs to do to take care of his mental state. She spends a day enjoying her own hobbies while her partner relaxes by himself. When they reunite at the end of the day, they feel refreshed after some alone time and happy to see each other.

Codependent: Partner B needs to destress alone but he's nervous to ask Partner A in case she takes it the wrong way. When he finally asks Partner A if they can have a day apart, she looks sad but begrudgingly allows him to go. While they're away from each other, they are anxious. Partner B starts to feel guilty for leaving Partner A and he thinks to himself that it was a bad idea. When they reunite at the end of the day, Partner A is sulky and tries to guilt trip Partner B for leaving. Feeling bad, Partner B feels he has to fix it and make it up to her.

Example #3

Dependent: Both partners express what they need to feel valued and taken care of in the relationship. Each person makes their thoughts and feelings known while the other listens closely and thinks of how they can best meet their partner's needs.

Codependent: Partner A expresses her needs while Partner B listens closely and tries to help. Partner A is seen as having more pressing needs since her emotional state is more fragile. Partner B may bring up his concerns, but this gets brushed aside since he believes fragile Partner A has more important needs. Partner A silently agrees that her needs are more important.

It can be exceedingly difficult for people to admit to codependence. The fact of the matter is that codependent partners often have pure intentions at heart; they simply want to help their significant others and ease their suffering. Still, the results are no less counterproductive. In most cases, the dynamic does far more harm than good to both partners involved. If you think you might be in a codependent relationship, it's vital that you recognize this as soon as possible.

Signs You're the Enabler in a Codependent Relationship

The caretaker or 'giver' in a codependent relationship is also called the 'enabler.' This is because, through excessive care, they are enabling their partner's self-destructive behavior. If you tick three or more of the following boxes, then you are most likely the enabler in your relationship.

• You Constantly Give In

When your partner needs or wants something, you always find yourself giving in and doing what they want. Sometimes it will feel unreasonable and you may even resent them for it – but you continue to give in anyway. You end up dismissing your feelings to take care of your partner or keep the peace.

• You Take Responsibility for Their Actions

When a needy partner does something wrong or displays negative behavior, a codependent may find themselves taking responsibility for it. Instead of seeing their partner as the sole person at fault, they will believe they influenced that behavior. Codependent givers constantly make excuses for their partners and they may even blame themselves for it.

• You Perform Simple Tasks They Should Be Doing for Themselves

It's normal to care for our partners, but how often are you required to help with simple tasks that every other adult can accomplish just fine? Are you the person that gets your partner fed? Do you constantly have to wake them up so they aren't late to appointments? Do you end up finishing the chores that they were supposed to handle?

• You're Always Trying to Fix Everything

113

You just can't help it. No matter what happens, you're always trying to meet needs that may or may not exist. If your partner isn't feeling his or her best, you feel like it's your responsibility to make them feel better. You may find yourself anticipating their needs and perhaps even trying to fix something that doesn't need to be fixed. In any case, whenever your partner needs anything, you're always there doing everything you can to make it better, even when they're not doing anything to help their own self.

• You Frequently Have to Ask for Your Partner's Approval

For one reason or another, you don't feel like you can do as you please. If you want to make a decision for yourself or have some time away, you feel like you need to check if your partner is okay with this. The reason behind this behavior is likely that you feel your partner may need you and the idea of your partner being alone makes you feel guilty. By getting your partner's approval, this guilt is eliminated.

• You See Your Partner as Helpless

Be honest with yourself here. Imagine your partner being left to their own devices for a whole week. Perhaps you're going away on an important trip to a place with minimal phone reception. Your partner will have to do everything on their own and look after him or herself without any outside help at all. How worried does this thought make you? Do you trust that your partner will be able to take care of him or herself and function properly without you? Will they be able to stay away from their bad habits, eat and sleep well, and get to important appointments on time? If you answered no to any of these questions, admit it to yourself: you believe your partner is helpless.

• When You're Not Taking Care of Your Loved One, You Feel Like a Bad Partner

At the end of the day, you continue giving and enabling because the alternative makes you feel guilty. You worry that if you set any boundaries, this will make matters worse for your partner. You feel that your partner really needs you and the thought of not helping them with everyday activities feels akin to tossing them overboard into the ocean. You are used to providing assistance and when you don't, you feel like you've done something terrible.

Are you in Denial?

One of the major obstacles in codependent relationships is denial. It is a core symptom of codependency. Even with expert advice right in front of you, nothing will help your situation if you can't admit there's something wrong. One of the reasons codependency is allowed to continue is because both partners are in denial about their unhealthy cycle. Before dysfunctions can be treated, it's essential that both partners stop living in denial about their bad habits or the severity of their effects. These are the signs you've been living in denial.

- **You dismiss your own feelings and instincts**

It's happened before. You've felt something nudge at your mind, saying, "It shouldn't be like this" or "This doesn't feel quite right." Instead of delving deeper into the issue, you always decide to brush this feeling aside. You tell yourself it isn't important or that the feeling is outright silly, even though this isn't the first time you've felt this way. If you often find yourself having to dismiss your instincts, thoughts, or feelings, then there's a good chance you're in denial. If a feeling continues to resurface, chances are that your intuition is correct.

- **You're just waiting for change**

Perhaps you've admitted to yourself that there needs to be change. What happens after that admission? Do you and your partner take action to remedy the situation immediately? Or do you just sit back and tell yourself it'll change with time? Relying on external influences or other people to change is another red flag you're in denial, especially if you've been 'waiting' for a rather long time. This shows you've given up your power to create change. Instead of making progress yourself, you are waiting for it to fall from the sky. People who do this tend to be in denial about how bad their situation is.

• Everyone sees a problem you don't see

Are there people in your life who insist your relationship is deeply flawed? The more people who have said this to you, the higher the likelihood that they're correct. If you can't see this problem, you're probably in denial about its existence. When we're entrenched in a dysfunctional pattern, sometimes it can be difficult to point it out. People on the outside of your relationship, however, can see the big picture. And the people who are close to you will know you best and what is best for you. If you constantly find yourself defending your relationship to close friends and family, there's a chance you're in denial that what they're saying is true.

Denial protects us from a harsh truth. By pretending not to notice something, we feel there's a possibility we can ignore it out of existence. This could not be further from the truth and in fact, denial can cause more harm than good. If you want to continue healing your relationship, nip your denial in the bud right now. Change only comes when you face reality.

Chapter 2: Understanding Codependent Personalities

What many people fail to realize is that it takes two dependent personalities to create a codependent relationship. These personalities are distinct but equally as problematic as each other. Those on the outside of the relationship have a tendency to blame whichever person is the most needy, but the fact of the matter is it's not just one person's fault. Both personalities carry their own dysfunctional traits, they just manifest in very different ways. When they come together, the worst instincts of these personalities are enabled. One partner's unhealthy behavior is exactly what the other person needs to indulge their own unhealthy behavior. This is how the codependent cycle begins and why it's often difficult to stop.

In order to create a healthier dynamic, it's essential that couples reflect on their individual selves. By now, it should be clear which of the two distinct roles each person in the relationship plays. This identification is step one. When both parties are aware of the role they play in the dynamic, there can finally come a greater understanding of what each person can do to heal the problem. It is important that both personalities are regarded with equal importance. To start making progress, both personalities should be studied and understood. It all starts with you.

Decoding the Enabler

At some point in the enabler's childhood, they were made to believe their needs are always secondary. In early studies of codependency, it was believed that enabling tendencies stemmed from growing up with an alcoholic parent, but today, experts agree there can be many causes. Alcoholic or not, these issues are usually the result of a needy or otherwise unavailable parent. While it is possible that the enabler was subjected to emotional or physical abuse, this is not always the case. Often, they simply grew up amidst highly dysfunctional family dynamics, and this may or may not involve a physically or mentally ill family member. These codependents did not receive adequate emotional care so they became accustomed to having their needs unmet. Most children grow up receiving a lot of positive validation; in the case of the enabler, they likely did not receive much validation at all. This results in an individual who, by default, does not feel very important. Instead, they've learned to find validation vicariously through someone else.

In the case of a needy or ill family member, the enabler may have had some caretaking responsibilities, thus solidifying their comfort in assuming a caretaking role later on in life. Whatever their childhood story, one thing is absolutely certain: the codependent has been taught their worth and value are directly linked to how much they please others and how well they can take care of other people. This flawed belief is exactly what creates dysfunction in this personality type. In an effort to feel worthy and good about themselves, they will seek out situations where they offer some form of help. The most wounded enablers may even feel that the more lost the cause, the bigger the reward. This can lead them into disastrous relationships, creating severe trauma, and only worsening the dysfunction. Still, many of these deeply wounded enablers continue to try and serve, believing that the problem lies with them and not their partner. It is a vicious cycle that only ends when self-awareness comes.

It's important to note that some enablers act from deep abandonment issues where they feel they must do everything to make their partner happy otherwise they will be abandoned. 'Abandonment' here does not necessarily mean a break-up. If the enabler suffered through the death of a sick parent, they may overhelp their sick partner, fueled by the subconscious fear that they'll have the same experience all over again.

If you're an enabler seeking recovery, it's vital that you figure out where this need to overhelp stems from. At what point in your life were you taught your needs were less important? Who was the person whose needs took priority over your own? Once you've identified this essential detail, you can begin to separate that incident from your current relationship.

Understanding the Enabled Partner

When studying codependent relationships, the enabled individual can be far more difficult to decode. Why? Because, while all enablers possess similar endgames and intentions, their enabled counterparts can have wildly different motives and causes. Many grew up being coddled or spoilt as children, so they started to expect the same treatment from other people close to them. But the flip side is also possible – they may have been neglected as children, causing them to turn to attention-seeking behaviors. If they were coddled as children, it's possible they don't recognize the reality of their situation. They may think it is completely normal to be waited on hand and foot because that's how they've been treated all their lives.

Many enabled individuals suffer from an addiction, a physical ailment, or a mental health condition. Instead of making steps towards recovery, they became far too comfortable or even started to enjoy being in a position where they had to be taken care of. Due to the overhelping tendencies of the enabler, they are never required to help themselves. In a person suffering from a physical affliction, this may mean they refuse to get up and retrieve things for themselves, even if they are fully capable. Or they may start to expect others to cook for them, even if they have the strength and resources to do so for themselves. Or they may take an extended leave from work, insisting they are too sick or unwell, even if all evidence shows they are perfectly fine.

Since their backgrounds can vary wildly, it is important to examine their childhood. Look at their relationship with their primary caregivers. Were they spoilt in some way or were they outright neglected? Here are some case studies to better help you understand the background of the enabled partner.

Case Studies

To protect the privacy of the people involved, no real names have been used.

- Mary remembers feeling neglected in her childhood. Her little brother suffered from a myriad of health complications as soon as he was brought home from the hospital. Naturally, he got more attention from their parents. She remembers being all alone with her nanny for days at a time while her parents stayed at the hospital with her sick brother. Eventually, her brother got better, but the dynamic was always the same, with him receiving far more attention than her. When she was a teenager, she admits to exaggerating symptoms of an illness because she wanted to get more attention from her parents. This plan succeeded. Suddenly, her parents began giving her the same attention they used to only give her brother. Worried she would become 'ignored' again, she continued to act helpless and sick because she learned that this was the best way to get others to care for her. Eventually, Mary entered a codependent relationship. Her partner went above and beyond to help her because he believed she was very ill and unable to look after herself. To break this codependency, Mary had to learn that there were other more fulfilling ways to receive affection from people.

- For as long as John can remember, he was always given whatever he wanted. He came from an extremely privileged family and he was never required to lift a finger to do anything. He didn't even recognize what a position of privilege he was in; he just thought it was completely normal. If he needed something, there was always a helper available or his parents could easily pay for a solution. In addition to this privilege, he was also an only child with no one to fight over attention for. His mother, in particular, coddled him and he enjoyed being coddled. Eventually, he got into a codependent relationship with a person who grew up taking care of an alcoholic father. Naturally, she became John's enabler. She allowed him to do nothing, taking care of his every need while he took care of financial responsibilities with family money, but nothing else. When they eventually had children, John's partner found herself exhausted and stretched thin. He never helped her with anything and instead still expected her to help him too. Since John was very used to a female enabler being in his life, it was difficult for him to realize that he had deep-set codependent ways.

As demonstrated, enabled partners can be raised in wildly different ways. What they always have in common, however, is that they're taught to equate affection and love with being treated as helpless. In Mary's case, she started to feel that the only way to get attention from her parents was by being sick. In the case of John, he felt that overhelping and being coddled *was* love because of how his parents, especially his mother, treated him. At some point along the way, the lines became blurred with their primary caregiver.

To help the enabled partner in your relationship, see if you can identify where these feelings originated in their childhood. Is your partner more of a Mary or more of a John?

Narcissistic & Borderline Personality Disorder

When dealing with Narcissistic and Borderline Personality Disorder, emotional and psychological abuse are usually at work. Individuals with these personality disorders are always in the enabled position, never the enabler. The codependency becomes infinitely more toxic when these personalities are involved. Narcissists feel entitled to an obedient partner and may even enjoy watching the enabler stumble over them, trying to do everything they can to fulfill their every whim. Indeed, an enabler is a Narcissist's perfect partner. The Narcissist wants to feel special and like the whole world revolves around them, and there the enabler is showing them exactly that. The enabler of a Narcissist is often referred to as a 'Co-Narcissist.'

Borderline personalities can be equally damaging to the enabler; they are prone to feelings of betrayal and abandonment. In the Borderline personality, the enabler sees a victim they can finally save. The Borderline personality wants a hero or savior and it comes naturally for the enabler to play that part. Unfortunately, what the enabler fails to realize is that this is part of the Borderline personality's destructive pattern. They will never truly be the hero in the story because the Borderline will always feel betrayed and abandoned over something. The emotional instability inherent in this personality disorder means the enabler will never succeed in their attempt to save. The Borderline personality has issues that are solely their own problem to solve – the enabler must recognize this as soon as possible.

It is much more difficult for someone with a personality disorder to change. Unless these partners are self-aware and committed to self-transformation, there is a high likelihood they will continue to engage in their usual pattern. And with a Narcissist or Borderline personality, this pattern can be highly destructive. If you're an enabler to one of these personality types, reconsider your involvement in the relationship or invest in couples therapy.

Dependent Personality Disorder

The most common personality disorder found in codependent relationships is – you guessed it – the Dependent Personality Disorder. Those with this personality disorder may fall into either the enabler or enabled position. Dependent personalities are inclined to feel anxiety and fear when they are by themselves. Naturally, they turn to other people to fulfill all their emotional and psychological needs. Without approval, validation, or help from other people, Dependents feel like a fish out of water.

At their most severe, Dependent personalities may have a hard time functioning in their daily lives without something present. This can lead them to shirk responsibilities and become completely passive. When left on their own, they can feel extremely helpless. As you'd expect, Dependent personalities take break-ups harder than the average individual. They may feel utterly devastated until they find someone else to take their ex-partner's place. When an enabler suffers from this disorder, they may be extremely competent while in a relationship but feel there's 'no point' if they don't have someone.

This disorder does not just affect the romantic sphere of the Dependent's life. In fact, everyone who knows the individual will experience their dependency. Friends, family, and perhaps even coworkers and bosses will see this side of the Dependent.

5 Types of Dependent Personalities

Renowned psychologist, Theodore Millon, can be credited with identifying the five distinct types of dependent personalities in adults. While all Dependents will share similar traits, each type will display its own unique behavior and strategies for getting what they want. If you believe either you or your partner have Dependent Personality Disorder, see if you can figure out which type they are. It is possible to have symptoms belonging to a few different types but there is usually just one that dominates.

- **The Disquieted Dependent**

The Disquieted subtype is wrought with anxiety and restlessness. They fear abandonment from the people around them and feel intense loneliness when they are not with a supportive figure. Feelings of inadequacy run rampant and they are often very sensitive to rejection.

- **The Immature Dependent**

Dependents under this subtype have a tendency to be childlike, especially in the face of everyday responsibilities. Despite being an adult, they will find it difficult to cope with typical adult expectations. The Immature type needs a significant amount of 'babying' as they can be naive and lacking in general life skills.

- **The Accommodating Dependent**

This type is characterized by extreme benevolence and, as its name suggests, a tendency to be over-accommodating. These individuals strive to please others and will come across as incredibly agreeable. Naturally, they take on a submissive role and reject all uncomfortable feelings. These types may be very gracious and neighborly towards everyone around them.

- **The Selfless Dependent**

The Selfless subtype bears many similarities to the Accommodating subtype, but there is a stronger inclination to abandon their individual identity and merge it with another person's. When left unchecked, they'll become absorbed by another person and live as a mere extension of them. Of all the types, these Dependents are most likely to appear as not having a personality.

- **The Ineffectual Dependent**

Like the Immature Dependent, the Ineffectuals do not cope well with difficulties and responsibilities. The Ineffectuals will take it a step further, however, refusing to deal with anything at all that may be uncomfortable. A caretaker is essential for them to function in life. They are prone to fatigue and lethargy. They are unproductive and most of the time, highly incompetent. On occasion, Ineffectual Dependents may even struggle with feelings of empathy and instead be overcome by a general apathy towards their life, including any shortcomings.

No matter the subtype, all people suffering from this personality disorder can get better with therapy and committed self-work. In fact, many Dependent personalities have found healthy levels of independence after sufficient treatment. If you feel your codependence is linked to this disorder, rest assured that this condition does not have to dictate your life.

Common Wounds of Both Personalities

All dependent personalities may manifest varying behavior, but for the most part, they are rooted in similar psychological wounding. With the exception of some Narcissistic and Borderline Personality types, codependent individuals have low self-esteem and strong insecurities. At the end of the day, both partners feel they desperately need each other in order to feel complete. The only difference is it takes different types of behavior to achieve this sense of completion – a feeling that never lasts long because it is always up to someone else to fill this need.

By nature, Dependent personalities have trouble forming and distinguishing their own identity. They don't know who they truly are and they have a low sense of personal value. When asked about their core strengths, many will find themselves at a loss for what to say unless they receive feedback from someone else. Their flawed and incomplete sense of identity is exactly why they quickly latch onto other people. They see this other person as a kind of mirror image. Any uncertainty they feel inside is solved by looking to this other person and merging with them.

To eliminate the Dependent's tendency to attach themselves to another person, it is vital that they learn some level of independence. They must experience the world without a crutch to walk on their own. Their family, friends, and partners must learn to give them healthy boundaries and a healthy level of support. Without challenges, they cannot improve and grow into their strength. Codependency is a quick and easy way to placate a deep wound, but it is never a long-term or lasting solution.

Understanding the Anxious Attachment Style

When it comes to understanding one's approach to relationships, attachment styles can shed a lot of light on why certain people behave the way they do. Quite simply, our attachment style shows us how we go about getting what we want and the strategies we use to meet our needs. Our varying approaches are determined by our childhoods, specifically our relationship with our primary caregiver. If you had an emotionally unavailable parent or one that abandoned you in some way, this will affect the way you behave in all future relationships.

The Anxious attachment style is one of three dominant styles and is the one most commonly found in codependent individuals. The Anxious type is formed when an individual experiences trauma during the developmental period of their life. For one reason or another, their 'safe space' was upturned or destroyed. Their sense of physical or emotional safety was compromised in a significant way and it may have resulted in a life-altering breach of trust. This traumatic incident likely involved abandonment, violence, emotional abuse, or other forms of trauma.

As its name suggests, the Anxious type has developed a deep sense of anxiety in response to relationships and intimacy. Whether they show it or not, there is a hypervigilance for signs of abandonment fueled by an intense fear of being left behind in some way. These types crave intimacy and may even fantasize about the 'perfect partner' while single. In relationships, they may resort to manipulation or playing games during times of deep insecurity. They are more inclined to be pessimistic, imagining the worst outcome especially in regards to their close relationships.

The Anxious type is most likely to end up in a codependent relationship because they have a tendency to put their partner's needs before their own. Since abandonment is seen as the worst possible outcome, they naturally strive for the opposite extreme. In the eyes of the Anxious type, codependency is a sign of deep love and unmatched intimacy. The idea of anything less scares them. Codependency allows them to feel like they have 'tabs' on everything happening in the relationship. This is a coping mechanism for their abandonment issues. The closeness of codependency grants them the illusion of having total control.

The most tight-knit codependencies are formed by two people with this same attachment style. It should be noted, however, that not all people possessing this attachment style will present signs of the same severity. As with everything, all people are on a spectrum. Those with severe Anxious inclinations will need to work harder on breaking their destructive patterns.

At the end of the day, whichever type or attachment style you possess, the lessons that must be learned are the same. If you saw your or your partner's behavior reflected in these pages, don't feel discouraged over getting called out. Just focus on the lessons at hand and you'll soon find yourself evolving from your codependent ways.

Chapter 3: For the Love of Boundaries

Whenever the words 'boundaries' or 'limitations' come into the conversation, it is always associated with negative connotations. People tend to think that boundaries will lead to some form of deprivation and that all enjoyment will be stripped from their lives forevermore. This is, of course, a ridiculous notion. Boundaries keep us sane and safe. They are akin to the walls of a house, keeping a healthy barrier between what's ours and what's *out there.* Boundaries and walls don't mean that we live in isolation or loneliness; it simply means we start gaining better control over our thoughts, feelings, and spaces. Without boundaries, the world and our lives would be chaos. Start seeing the beauty in boundaries. Would you want to live in a house with no walls? I'll bet not.

One key thing that all codependents struggle with is – you guessed it! – boundaries. Their tendency to merge identities with another individual means that they no longer embrace their independence. They start to perceive separation and individuality as negative ideas. Boundaries are uncomfortable and difficult to put in place because any separation poses a threat to their peace of mind. They see it as being alone indefinitely instead of healthy and temporary space apart. Whether you realize it or not, your relationship desperately needs boundaries. Avoiding temporary discomfort now could to lasting frustration in the future. Perhaps even a ruined relationship. Many couples who allow this to happen look back in regret, wishing they'd been strong when it mattered the most. Don't let that happen to you and your relationship.

To start healing your codependency, a necessary step is to start working on healthier boundaries and the mindset it takes to make them successful.

5 Vital Ways to Build Strong Self-Awareness

Before boundaries can be established, it's important that you recognize what your needs are and, most importantly, which needs are not currently being met. This requires self-awareness. As a codependent, some of your needs will be difficult to admit to. In fact, you may even find yourself outright disagreeing. Whenever the urges to disagree or fight back arise, consider whether this response is really rooted in your needs or whether you're only reacting out of fear. It is highly common for codependents to fear the challenge of independence. To achieve growth and true happiness, however, it's essential that you embrace this challenge. Self-awareness will keep you grounded and alert about what you need to feel fully satisfied.

1. Write Down Your Thoughts

Try to make a habit of writing down your feelings and thoughts. Notice when an emotion arises and take note of what brings this up. This time to focus on your mind will train you to be more in tune with what you feel and think. Sometimes we don't notice because we never take the time to really experience our inner world. Make sure that whatever you write doesn't fully revolve around your partner. Focus on what *you* feel. Write about other spheres of your life or topics that interest you in the greater world. Feel free to write in a journal or just in a Word document on your computer. Wherever you choose to write, the benefit is the same.

2. Visualize Your Ideal Self

The best part about this exercise is that you can do it anywhere, anytime, and it can take as little as a few minutes. For the best results, however, we advise doing it in the early morning or right before bedtime as this is when your mind is likely to be less agitated. Close your eyes and start to form a mental picture of your future self. What does your ideal self look like? What has he or she accomplished that you're proud of? What are your ideal self's biggest strengths? How does he or she act in the face of life's challenges? Now, imagine that this ideal self is actually who you're looking at in the mirror. You already are your ideal self. Embrace the strengths you wish to have. They are already in you waiting to be unlocked.

Not only does this exercise empower you but it also allows you to see what your true values are. And most importantly, it allows you to reconnect with your dreams and your purpose. Needless to say, while performing this exercise, it's important that you keep all your visualizations strictly about you and not involved with your partner.

3. Ask Someone for Feedback

The thought of asking someone for feedback can seem terrifying but it's one of the best ways to receive an honest insight. Make sure to choose someone who knows you reasonably well and whose opinion you trust. Also, make sure whoever you talk to will be capable of staying constructive. Steer clear of anyone in your life who is overly critical or unkind. You can do this in person, over the phone or even by email. Ask this person what they feel your strengths are and where they think your areas for growth are. When you receive that feedback, think it over. Embrace your strengths and also look at your areas for growth in a level-headed, practical manner. When moving forward with your personal growth, try and work on these areas the best you can.

4. Take Different Personality Tests

Whether it's the Myers-Briggs test, a SWOT analysis, or an Enneagram quiz, try and have fun with some different personality tests. The goal here is to get to know yourself a little better and solidify your sense of self. Not only will these tests give you new insights into your personality attributes, they will also point out strengths you may have never considered before. Identifying your Myers-Briggs and Enneagram type will aid you in putting your needs into words, and they'll give you a much better idea of where you'll need to set some boundaries. If you discover that you're deeply introverted, you may realize that alone time and solitude is very important to you. Or perhaps it's the opposite and you realize it's more social time with friends that you desperately need in your life. Take these newly identified needs into account and plan on making them a priority in your brand new non-codependent chapter.

5. Monitor Your Inner Dialogue

Every single person engages in self-talk and, even if we don't realize, we are strongly influenced by the manner in which we speak to ourselves. Pay attention to your inner dialogue when faced with different events and decisions. When you do something wrong, what does the voice in your head say? When you do something right, do you give yourself the positive encouragement you deserve or do you give someone else the credit? Take note of the patterns in your inner dialogue. Notice when you're being harsh on yourself.

Instead of putting yourself down for failures, try to be constructive and show yourself compassion. If you can, think of a solution instead of a put-down. If you forgot to pay your phone bill again, don't dwell on your forgetfulness. Be kind to yourself; perhaps you've been stressed or working hard at something else. What can you do to prevent this from happening in the future? Perhaps, you could create reminders on your phone or leave brightly colored post-it notes on the fridge. Try dwelling on the solution instead of the problem.

"So, Where Exactly Should I Draw the Line?"

Using the ideas in the previous section, you might have come up with a few ideas for boundaries you can set. I highly encourage you to run with these and make them happen! If you still don't have any clear ideas, don't worry. You're codependent and you may not be accustomed to thinking in terms of yourself yet. Here are some ideas for where you can draw some boundaries:

1. Time Together

In codependent relationships, it's very common for both partners to spend an exorbitant amount of time together. This is a good place to start when you're thinking of where to draw boundaries. If you see each other everyday, suggest spending one or two days apart to focus on your individual hobbies. If you live together, this may mean taking the day out in different areas and only seeing each other in the evenings. If it isn't realistic to spend whole days apart, consider modifying your daily routine so you spend a few hours in a secluded area of the house.

2. Household Chores

It's very common for the enabler to take on most of the household chores. They are, after all, the more active partners in the relationship. A great way to establish more balance in your dynamic is by adding more fairness to your household duties. This aspect of living with a partner is easily overlooked but it is a huge signifier of balance or imbalance in the relationship. If you tend to do most or all of the chores, tell your partner you will no longer bear most of the burden. Insist on doing half of the chores each. If you're inclined to be more gentle on them, you could even let them choose which chores they would prefer to do. Make sure you stick to this new arrangement by giving them frequent reminders or putting up a chore roster.

3. Bad Habits

This is a big one in codependent relationships. The enabled partners always have some bad habit that is creating strain in the relationship. It could be something as major as a drug addiction or something less major like general laziness. Drawing boundaries around bad habits is essential in a codependent relationship, especially if it's affecting you in some way. Be firm with this boundary, but also think of ways you can support them through this boundary. If you need your partner to go to AA meetings, consider being the person to drive them to each meeting. If you want your partner to get a job, help them look for jobs and put together a dazzling resume. If there are little habits that bother you, consider drawing boundaries there as well. Don't like it when your partner leaves his dirty socks on the sofa? Start setting that boundary!

4. Verbal Communication: Language & Tone

Verbal communication is a difficult one to master and it's possible your partner has tendencies that really irk you. Maybe even more than that – maybe you find them hurtful and upsetting. If your partner speaks to you in a way that you find bothersome, don't hesitate to call it out, especially if they call you names, raise their voice, mock you, or belittle you in moments of anger. Boundaries around counterproductive communication styles can be more difficult to implement since these decisions are made in the spur of the moment, but I'm willing to bet that until now you haven't fought back. Just calling it out and telling your partner you will no longer tolerate it can be enough to put a stop to it.

5. Decisions and Making Plans

If one person in your relationship consistently takes on a dominant role, it's likely that person makes most of the decisions. Some of these may include what activities to partake in, what to eat, where to go, and who to see. If your partner tends to get his or her way when it comes to making plans, try and point this fact out. Draw boundaries around how often they can dominate your shared plans. Suggest sharing this decision or allocating certain days to your choice and your partner's choice. And if it's you that tends to dominate, have the strength to create this balance in your relationship. If your partner shrugs the decision off and asks you to choose every single time, insist that they choose. They may be hesitant but later on, knowing they made this decision will empower them in their own life.

6. How to Spend Money

This decision is another big one. A lack of boundaries around finances can lead to a lot of resentment for couples who don't learn to work together. In a codependent relationship, there's a high likelihood one partner is spending more money than the other or putting it towards something that is destructive to their own lifestyle. Perhaps you have a partner that is spending all your money on shopping and you just can't say no. Or perhaps he or she is using it to pay for their bad habits. If money is going towards a counterproductive activity or habit, start drawing boundaries here. There are always better things to invest in. Bring up your future together. Think of all the money you could have saved for a new house, a new TV, or even a vacation together. Come together to draw boundaries on how money gets spent and how much; you won't regret it!

4 Questions to Eliminate Guilt Before Setting Boundaries

Whenever codependent partners are faced with the thought of boundary-setting, they inevitably bring up the guilt they feel. This all goes back to the unhealthy notion that boundaries are unkind. Codependent people feel that this is equivalent to slapping their partner's hand away or telling them to back off. Let's clear this up right now: boundary-setting is not rejection! When done properly, no feelings are hurt and everyone wins. A lack of boundaries can lead to people feeling resentment or frustration down the road – and this can do real damage to a romantic partnership.

While it's completely normal for codependent people to have hesitation about setting boundaries, they need to recognize this feeling must be overcome. If the thought of setting boundaries with your partner makes you feel uncomfortable, that's okay! This is just further proof that you really are codependent. The good news is this guilt can be eliminated with some self-reflection. Now, let's get working!

- **"How is my lack of boundaries holding me back from my dreams and goals?**
  After utilizing the suggestions in the 'Self-Awareness' section, think about the path between where you are now and the goals you want to achieve. Whether you realize it or not, your lack of boundaries is creating an obstacle. How exactly does this obstacle manifest itself?

134

This doesn't have to be your big life dream, it can also be your short-term goals. For example, let's say you've been wanting to start working out so you can get in better shape. If you aren't creating boundaries around money and time, this leaves less available to achieve this goals. If you're buying your codependent partner anything he or she wants, and spending every minute of every day with them, how are you going to afford a membership at a great gym? How will you find the time or energy to start working out? Reflect on how satisfying it would be to finally achieve these goals. Wouldn't it be a shame if you let your relationship get in the way? How will you feel later on in life when you realize your chance is over?

- **"In what ways will I feel more positive after I set these boundaries?"**

Imagine how it'll feel after you successfully set these boundaries. You don't have to name these feelings if you don't want to. Just experience it mentally and emotionally. Try to put yourself in the shoes of your future self. It could be a few weeks or months down the road – whenever your boundaries have been able to reap their full benefits. If you're setting boundaries to get more time to yourself, think of all the things you'll accomplish with that time. Imagine how it'll make you feel to see how much you've achieved because you had the strength to set those boundaries. If you're considering adding more rules to the way money is spent, imagine having all that extra money in the future. What will you do with it? Think of the many wonderful things you can put your saved money towards! Imagine taking a fantastic vacation with your partner because you were finally able to restrict their terrible spending habits!

- **"In what ways will my partner grow if I set these boundaries?"**

You think you're helping by not drawing boundaries, but this could not be further from the truth. Let's examine that flawed belief for a moment. What exactly makes you think you're helping by letting them do as they please? Is it because in that moment you're not causing them discomfort or displeasure? Why is short-term displeasure the enemy and not long-term frustration or dissatisfaction? People grow through challenges. As a partner, it's not your job to eliminate all challenges; it's your job to make sure your partner has the necessary support through their life challenges. Support means staying by their side not sacrificing your well-being.

What will your partner improve through these new boundaries? How will they grow? If you're trying to help your partner quit a bad habit, think of the growth they'll see once they finally let it go. Perhaps they'll have better health, more money, and more time to focus on their goals. They may learn to be more patient, more empowered, and they may even start to be a better partner towards you.

- **"How will my relationship be stronger after better boundaries?"**

With the answers to all the other questions in mind, reflect on the overall impact these boundaries will have on your relationship. You've now identified the ways in which you will feel more positive and the growth your partner will see; what does this mean for your relationship as a whole? Your relationship may be comfortable now, but what if your relationship was empowering instead? Imagine what you'd be able to accomplish together.

Essential Tips for Setting Healthy Boundaries Successfully

1. Add Boundaries as Seamlessly As Possible

Here's a pro tip for setting boundaries with positive outcomes: weave them in seamlessly and do not make a big deal out of them. A rookie mistake that new boundary-setters make is approaching the topic with a heavy, sad air and infusing too much intensity into the conversation. There's no need to treat it this way! If want to reserve a day each week for working out, just say, "Hey honey, I'm going to start focusing on getting fit. I've been dying to get in shape! I'm thinking of making Saturday my solo work-out day. You're going to love my new hot bod - just wait!" Notice how casual and lighthearted this is. By bringing new changes up this way, it doesn't feel scary and serious. It's just a small new change - no big deal! Your partner is less likely to worry and you'll see for yourself how incredibly normal it sounds to draw boundaries.

2.

se Positive Language

If you're trying to suggest more time apart, do *not* say, "Darling, I think we need to spend more time apart. It's driving me crazy and I can't handle it anymore." This negative and emotional language will worry your partner. Remind yourself that this isn't a negative event, it's quite the opposite. Your relationship is evolving. Be positive and excited for your new chapter. If you're discussing your new boundaries with your partner, infuse the conversation with positive language. Focus on the benefits you'll see instead of how difficult it's going to be.

3. Assure Your Partner

Needless to say, the first conversation you have about boundaries may incite a little bit of anxiety in your partner. Expect this and don't let it discourage you. When it happens, assure and remind your partner that the reason you want these boundaries is because you want to improve your relationship. Why? Because you love your partner and you want to ensure both your happiness for the future to come. When your partner appears worried, continue to bring up this fact. Inaction is a greater signifier of our apathy in a relationship; if you're actively trying to make improvements, this is evidence that you really care about the future of your relationship.

4. Stay Firm & Do Not Waver

Since boundaries are new to your relationship, it's possible that there will be some pushback from your partner. Prepare in advance for how you'll respond. Whatever you do, stay firm in your assertions and do not back down. If you appear ambivalent or uncertain, this will only add to your partner's hesitation. Remain confident and you'll eventually convince your partner that this is the best course of action. If your partner is prone to manipulation or guilt-tripping, make further preparations for these tactics. See if you can guess how they'll resist and come up with an effective comeback. Keep the benefits of your boundaries in mind and do not allow them to pull you back into your old destructive patterns.

5. Do Not Make Threats

If your partner disrespects the boundaries you've aligned, it's important that there are some consequences for this – but only handle this outcome when it occurs. Do not make threats in anticipation of this event. For the moment, try to believe that your partner will take these boundaries seriously. As soon as threats enter the conversation, you start veering off into emotionally abusive territory. It is absolutely essential that your partner starts making changes out of love for you and your relationship, and not fear for the consequences you've threatened them with. Threatening them will infuse a lot of negativity into the situation and it will only worsen the codependence.

6. Emphasize Change on Both Sides

If you want your partner to cooperate, avoid making it sound like they are the only person who needs to change. Remember, you're both co-creating this situation. As we established in the previous chapter, it takes two personalities to form codependency. Even if you feel like your partner has more work to do, it's important that you take accountability for your actions as well. Tell them what you're going to do as your part in this new change. Your partner will be far more likely to respond positively if you make it sound like this is a journey you're embarking on together. Do not pin the responsibility solely on them.

7. Abide by Your Own Rules

If you're going to draw boundaries in your relationship then you, too, must respect them. How can you expect your partner to take them seriously if you don't? It is completely unfair to ask your partner to change and then not do your own self-work. If you're trying to restrict your partner's drug habit, then it's only fair you control your alcohol dependence. A good rule of thumb is to treat every boundary you create for your partner as a boundary for yourself as well. Do not be a hypocrite. Keep the playing field level at all times and listen to your own rules. You help to set the tone for how seriously your boundaries can be taken.

Chapter 4: Developing Powerful Self-Esteem

A short message from the Author:

Hey! Sorry to interrupt. I just wanted to check in and ask if you're enjoying the Conversation Skills 2.0 audiobook? I'd love to hear your thoughts!

Many readers and listeners don't know how hard reviews actually are to come by, and how much they help an author.

So I would be incredibly thankful if you could take just 60 seconds to leave a quick review on Audible, even if it's just a sentence or two!

And don't worry, it won't interrupt this audiobook.

To do so, just click the 3 dots in the top right corner of your screen inside of your Audible app and hit the "Rate and Review" button.

This will take you to the "rate and review" page where you can enter your star rating and then write a sentence or two about the audiobook.

It's that simple!

I look forward to reading your review. Leave me a little message as I personally read every review!

Now I'll walk you through the process as you do it.

Just unlock your phone, click the 3 dots in the top right corner of your screen and hit the "Rate and Review" button.

Enter your star rating and that's it! That's all you need to do.

I'll give you another 10 seconds just to finish sharing your thoughts.

----- Wait 10 seconds -----

Thank you so much for taking the time to leave a short review on Audible.

I am very appreciative as your review truly makes a difference for me.

Now back to your scheduled programming.

The overall health of a relationship is dependent on the two individuals belonging to it. It is not its own entity. If you're a deeply insecure person, you're going to carry those insecurities into your relationship. If you're jealous while you're single, you're going to be a jealous partner as well. These issues don't just disappear as soon as someone else is in the picture. Expecting a relationship to fix you is another way that codependency forms. Partners cling to each other with hopes it'll diminish their inner turmoil, led to believe it's the ultimate cure. When it doesn't seem to work, they cling harder until the attempt backfires entirely. To be in a healthy relationship, you need to work on being a healthy individual. One way to do this is by working on your self-esteem. Believe it or not, broken self-esteem is often the root of many flawed relationship dynamics. This is no less true for codependencies.

The tips and exercises in this chapter will all contribute to a stronger sense of self and more powerful self-esteem. Take the time out to think of you and only you.

How High Self-Esteem Can Improve Your Codependency

Codependent partners tend to be in denial about the connection between self-esteem and codependency. Many insist that their codependency is born out of deep love and commitment for each other, but this is a delusion. Deep love and commitment may indeed exist but many couples are able to feel the same way without resorting to unhealthy patterns. One of the major differences is that healthy couples have higher levels of self-esteem. These are the improvements self-esteem can make to daily dynamics:

Example #1

Low Self-Esteem: You frequently doubt yourself and feel indecisive. This results in inaction about how to go about reaching your goals. You're not even sure if they're good goals to have. Overall, you feel overwrought with skepticism about your choices in life. This is why you rely on your partner to tell you what to do.

High Self-Esteem: When it comes to your goals, you trust that you can find the right course of action. This doesn't mean you won't make any mistakes along the way, but you trust that if you do, you'll discover how to fix the problem and do so accordingly. You listen to your partner's feedback but you never allow it to be the deciding vote, unless you agree.

Example #2

Low Self-Esteem: It feels like you do everything wrong. Every time you try to do something new, it always backfires and fails. You don't believe you have any strong abilities. You prefer it if your partner does everything because you can't do anything as well as they can. You believe yourself to be deeply incompetent.

High Self-Esteem: You may not do everything right all the time, but you know you're still a highly competent person. There's a learning curve for everyone and you always get it right eventually. You are completely comfortable taking care of your own self and are happy to share chores or other tasks with your partner since you know you can handle them just as well. No one's perfect but you know you can do anything you put your mind to.

Example #3

Low Self-Esteem: You're so afraid of being by yourself. This is why you can't implement any boundaries in your relationship; you're terrified it will cause your partner to leave you. Even when your partner does something that bothers you, you bite your tongue and keep your feelings to yourself. You just want to please them so that they stay with you. You don't know who you are without them and you're not sure how you'd go on by yourself. You desperately need them in your life to feel secure.

High Self-Esteem: Of course you love your partner - after all, that's why you're with them! - but you'll be okay if your relationship doesn't work out. You're in the relationship because you want your partner, not because you *need* your partner. You have no problem being honest and setting boundaries with your partner because you know what you need to be happy in a relationship. If your partner isn't willing to cooperate then that's a clear sign they aren't the right person for you. You know your worth and value outside of being in a couple. Your relationship consists of two whole people – not two halves.

Quit Codependency with these 22 Self-Esteem Affirmations

Positive affirmations are a proven way to improve one's self-talk. By reciting empowering mantras, your inner dialogue shifts and all self-sabotaging tendencies can be relinquished over time. To help build your self-esteem and solidify your inner confidence, try and make these positive affirmations part of your self-talk. Continued practice will rewire your brain to instantly feel more personal satisfaction.

1. Everything I need is already inside of me.
2. I am the master of my own emotions.
3. Today I will overcome obstacles with renewed strength.
4. I am my own fortress. I, alone, am in control of what enters and what leaves.
5. I can easily supply whatever I need.
6. I am capable of doing great things.
7. I let go of my past troubles and welcome brighter days.
8. I can stand proudly and courageously on my own.
9. I am open and ready to experience my true power.
10. Every step I take leads me to success.
11. I am fueled by my inner magic.
12. I am inhaling powerful confidence and exhaling self-doubt.
13. I am stronger than ever before.
14. I am whole and I am enough.
15. I am buzzing with brilliance.
16. Everything I touch becomes infused with light.
17. I am an unstoppable force.
18. I am an overflowing cup of love and joy.
19. I am fire and I am blazing ahead.
20. The universe supports me and all of my dreams.
21. Beauty is all around me and I create it wherever I go.
22. Today is the beginning of my best life chapter so far.

8 Exercises for Developing Powerful Self-Esteem

The greatest thing about self-esteem is that it can be built. How you feel about yourself now is not how you'll feel forever. The only reason you have low self-esteem is because your brain is used to creating negative thoughts about yourself – but it is in no way indicative of who you really are. It's time to break the pattern for good and start looking at yourself with kindness. You possess many positive qualities and it's time you start recognizing that.

1. The Journal of Wins

Your days are filled with wins. You may not realize it, but it's true. The reason you don't notice them is because you're waiting for a big win to fall out from the sky, but you accomplish small and medium wins every single day! These deserve to be celebrated too. Thing is, it isn't realistic to accomplish a big win every day. No one does that! To rev yourself up for a big win, start a journal and fill it with your little victories. Every day, list three things that you did right – both the intentional and unintentional wins. Did you make yourself an absolutely delicious sandwich? Did you spend less time on social media today than you did yesterday? Perhaps you gave a stranger a compliment and it made them noticeably happy? These are all wins to be celebrated!

2. Blame the Circumstances, Not the Individual

Whenever we make a mistake, we have a tendency to blame our personality. This isn't always fair. The next time you fail or make a mistake, try blaming the circumstances instead. For example, let's say you forgot to pick up groceries on your way home from work. Instead of calling yourself forgetful or stupid, try calling out the circumstances that got you here. Attribute this mistake to how busy you've been lately and the stress you've been feeling. You would have remembered to do the task if you weren't so tired! It's not who you are deep down inside. Now, it's important to not dwell on the mistake. Start thinking of solutions for next time, should the same circumstances arise.

3. Talk to Someone that Makes You Feel Great

How we feel about ourselves is strongly influenced by the people we're around. If you spend a lot of time with people who speak negatively about you or the world in general, you're going to absorb this negativity into your self-talk. If you can't eliminate everyone that makes you feel bad about yourself, make a point to also spend time with people that make you feel great. Spend time with them without bringing your partner along, if you can. Do they make you feel funny? Smart? Capable? Insightful? Lean into these good feelings and have fun with your new friend. And recognize that you truly are all these wonderful qualities that you feel!

4. Get Physical

Getting physical may sound like an odd way to build self-esteem but believe it or not, it works wonders. When we go on a hike or jog a couple of miles, we are faced with real evidence of our ability to accomplish something. We are simply doing and then succeeding. When we sit and stew in our own thoughts, it's easy for negativity and self-doubt to come flooding in. We need to get in the habit of simply *doing* and then looking back to see how far we've come. When we get active, we can put a distance to our progress or admire the view from our goal. It's a great way to remind ourselves of our power because we are *using* our power to give ourselves proof! The endorphins from getting active and the chance to remove yourself from your routine will also give you an immediate mood boost.

5. Respond to the Devil on your Shoulder

Some of us have an on-going relationship with the devil on our shoulder. It doesn't matter what we do, there's always a little voice telling us we're still not good enough. This voice may even convince us to stay away from any possible risk because we'll fail or we don't have the abilities to succeed. You've likely heard this voice before. However, I'll bet you normally listen and keep quiet when you hear it. From now on, you will not let this voice get away with making you feel bad. Even if it makes you feel crazy, respond to the devil on your shoulder. Fight, if necessary. Ask him what evidence he has to support what he's saying and throw conflicting evidence back at him. Think of how someone close to you would stick up for you in this situation.

6. Stand in a Power Pose

In a recent study, it was discovered that participants who stood in a power pose saw a decrease in their stress levels and an increase in their level of testosterone (which determines confidence). This is no surprise, of course, as body language is a known way of influencing our own state of mind. The next time you feel disempowered, sad, or low-energy, get yourself into one of these power poses for at least two minutes:

- Stand proudly with your legs apart and hands placed firmly on your hips. Make sure to push out your chest and straighten your back.
- Lean back in your chair and put your feet up on the table. Keep your hands folded behind your head and open out your chest.
- Lean back in your chair with your legs spread apart. Drape one arm over something that is next to you (such as a chair) feel free to do whatever you like with the other arm.

Try and avoid low-power poses by steering clear of crossing your arms, folding your hands, or hunching over in your seat. These will have the reverse effect. Choose a power pose and do it now!

7. Create an Alter Ego

Using an alter ego is a proven method for raising your confidence. In a study on mixed martial arts fighters, it was found that their creation of an alter ego helped to make them feel and perform better in the ring. Think of all the qualities you admire and start constructing a character that embodies all of these qualities. You can even think of a name for this character, if you like. The next time you're in a scenario where you feel shy or insecure, play this character. Ask yourself what this character would say if they were in this position and consider what they would do, how they would behave, etc. If you're taking this character out in public, try to not use their false name or give them a whole new life as it may be awkward if people find out you've been pretending. Make sure it's still you, but the 2.0 version of you. For a little extra fun, you can even play pretend that this character has a superpower. But this time, it's very important you don't try to show it off in public!

8. Treat Yourself Like a Loved One

The next time you catch yourself speaking negatively about who you are or what you've done, I want you to hold those thoughts. Now, instead of saying them to yourself, I want you to think of saying them to someone that you love. How would you feel if you heard someone speak that way to your loved ones? If it makes you feel angry or upset, this is the correct response. This should show you that negative self-talk is not the right way to talk to yourself either. If you want to give yourself criticism, think of how you'd give criticism to someone you really care about. You'd make it constructive and gentle, wouldn't you? Perhaps, you'd even take the time to remind them of their strengths. Imagine forming this constructive criticism for someone else and vow to only criticize yourself in this same gentle way.

Another alternative to this exercise is imagining your negative self-talk being directed at your child self. Do you know what you looked like when you were a little kid? A toddler, even? Can you imagine speaking so negatively to that small child? I'll bet you'd instantly start to feel bad. Again, form criticism as if you'd be speaking to this child self. This is the only right way to criticize yourself.

Chapter 5: Breaking Destructive Patterns

Codependent partners put up with a lot from each other and sometimes this includes a lot of destructive tendencies. Due to the clinging and enabling nature of codependencies, these habits and patterns are rarely dealt with in a proper manner. When the primary goal revolves around making your partner stay no matter what, a lot of problematic behavior gets swept under the rug. Then, denial sets in. Partners get too comfortable in the existing dynamic – so comfortable that incredibly unhealthy behavior is allowed to become normal. Chances are that your relationship, too, is filled with bad habits that need to be broken. You may not even be aware of their impact and the role they play in fueling the toxicity of your relationship. It doesn't matter how much work you do on your mentality; if your actions don't reflect that evolved mentality, it defeats the entire purpose of the self-work. There's no better time than now to end your destructive patterns.

5 Ways to Defeat Intense Jealousy

The clinging nature of a codependent relationship means that both partners, naturally, are afraid of the other person leaving them. This can often result in intense jealousy. One or both partners will look at people who they deem potential lovers of their significant other with heightened scrutiny. There's no telling who these 'potential lovers' will be identified as but whoever they are, the jealous partner will pull their significant other in the opposite direction. When jealousy is on overdrive, this can result in the isolation of both partners, since this is the only way they can assure their protection from individuals who make them jealous.

When jealousy and possessiveness are at their worst, there can also be jealousy over absolutely anyone that's close to the significant other in question. This can be friends and sometimes even family. The jealous partner feels the intense need to be the only one and does not want their 'special' closeness to be rivalled in any way. Needless to say, jealousy in any form can lead to destructive behavior, if left unchecked. While fleeting moments of jealousy are normal, they are considered serious when partners start taking action due to their jealousy. This can be anything like stalking this person on social media or trying to limit their time with our partner. Nip jealousy in the bud before it tears your relationship apart.

1. What if Your Roles Were Reversed?

During times of jealousy, we're essentially trying to guess how our partner feels in that moment. We don't have any facts, just uninformed guesses fueled by our insecurities. We're so hung up on thinking of our partner as a distant 'other' that we forget the terrible outcome we're imagining doesn't make that much sense.

Let's say you're at a party and there's an attractive person in the room. You suspect your partner is attracted to them and your mind is swarmed by awful thoughts where they leave you for this other person. Instead of continuing to picture this awful scenario, I want you to imagine a reverse scenario. What if there was an attractive person in the room that you were attracted to? What would be going through your head? How likely do you think it would be that you'd consider running off with this person and leaving your partner? Would you instantly forget your partner right then and there? The answer is probably no. What's more realistic is you'd notice this attractive person for a moment and then you'd move on with your life. This is most likely how it is for your partner as well. The next time you find yourself feeling jealous, ask yourself how you'd act if your roles were reversed.

2. Use Your Great Imagination to Your Advantage

Jealous people usually have fantastic imaginations. With very little information they can go off into their own little world and imagine the absolute worst outcome. The next time you catch yourself imagining the worst, I want you to try the opposite. I want you to use your imagination to think of the best case scenario instead. There's no reason this would be less likely than the worst case scenario! If your partner has an attractive coworker and you're imagining them falling in love while they work on a project together, stop right there and flip it around. Imagine your partner instead looking at this person and thinking about how much better looking you are. This may be the moment they realize 'Wow, I must really be in love with my partner because even though this other person is objectively attractive, I'm not attracted to him/her." What if, instead, your partner spends the whole time talking about you? These possibilities are just as likely. Why does it always have to be the worst?

3. Talk to Your Partner

Sometimes there's no better solution than just talking it out. Be honest with your partner and tell them how you feel about this other person. Jealous people jump to the worst conclusions and it's only when they hear their partner's feedback that they realize what a ridiculous assumption it was. Your partner may be able to clear up that no, he wasn't staring at that person because he was checking them out, he just thought that they looked an awful lot like their cousin. You never know until you bring it up. Your partner will reassure you that everything is alright and you'll quickly have your jealous feelings resolved. Only do this when your jealousy is really bothering you though, and avoid bringing it up every single time. Whenever you can, you should try and handle your thoughts on your own. Don't rely on your partner to fix everything for you.

4. Accept that Attraction is Normal

You could have the most loyal partner in the world who worships the ground you walk on – even this person is going to find some other people attractive. That's just how we're biologically wired. Attraction is completely normal. You can't stop it. As difficult as it is, you'll need to come to terms with this reality. Instead of feeling hurt by this human impulse, see if you can modify your psyche to just see it as a normal occurrence. Everyone feels attraction. Attraction is not a choice, it is just another feeling like hot, cold, hungry, or thirsty. Feelings of attraction are not the same as love and they are certainly not the same as cheating. As long as your partner isn't being disrespectful, it's no reason to punish them.

5. Remind Yourself that Feelings are Different from Actions
Jealous people get hung up on attraction like it's the same thing as cheating or flirting – but this could not be further from the truth. As we established in the previous point, attraction is a normal impulse. When you find yourself resenting your partner over their possible attraction towards someone, remind yourself that this is not an action they are taking. There's a difference between feeling hungry and gorging yourself on a feast. Someone might be thirsty but that's not the same as downing a jug of beer. Remind yourself that your partner hasn't taken any actions so there's no reason to feel upset or jealous.

6. Recognize that Your Feelings are a Reflection of You, Not Them
What people fail to realize is that their feelings about others are not indicative of anyone else's reality. Your jealousy is, in fact, a reflection of your own inner reality and your own insecurities. If you wish you were taller, you'll be jealous of tall people when, in fact, your partner may not care at all about this factor. A key step to defeating jealousy is to come to terms with this fact. Your feelings say more about you than anyone else. If you get hung up on an idea, it's likely to be more reflective of your insecurities as opposed to your partner's actual sense of attraction to someone else.

How to Break the Pattern
of Narcissistic Abuse

As we established in an earlier chapter, many narcissists end up in codependent relationships. Narcissists enjoy finding an enabler and unfortunately, many take pleasure in making them bend to their every whim. If you're currently in a codependent relationship with a narcissist or recovering from one, then there's a chance you've suffered through narcissistic abuse. Before we start breaking the pattern, it's important you understand how the narcissist cycle works:

- **STAGE ONE - The Pedestal**

When a narcissist is getting what they want or pleased with the way you treat them, they'll respond by putting you on a pedestal. At this stage, it can almost be difficult to believe the narcissist is truly a narcissist. They'll come across as sweet and loving, perhaps even attentive, as they try their best to conceal their dark side. For a short time, you'll feel as though you're on top of the world, like your narcissist partner really cherishes you. It's important to remember that they're only being so nice to you because they're getting what they want. Their goal is to encourage you to continue giving them what they want.

- **STAGE TWO - The 'Betrayal'**

As soon as the narcissist stops getting *exactly* their way, you'll see a completely different side of them. They may start to feel victimized, threatened or just outright offended. Often times, the trigger may seem completely harmless, though you'll start to recognize common triggers each time. It all comes down to what threatens their view that they are the center of the world. This can vary slightly with each narcissist. This perceived betrayal will push them into attack mode and can lead to much verbal abuse, lying, manipulation, accusations, and other forms of emotional abuse. This is where the narcissist is at his or her worst, actively trying to dominate and force the other person into submission.

- **STAGE THREE - The Discard**

How the narcissist acts at this stage depends on the response they receive in stage two. If they find it acceptable, they'll stop being aggressive. Instead, there may be mind games like the silent treatment. Without being aggressive or overt, the narcissist will start planting the seeds for stage one again. If the narcissist is not pleased with how you responded to them (and sometimes there's no telling what will trigger this) they will discard you, all for not putting up with their terrible behavior. They'll do this while making you out to be the villain while they're, of course, the victim. It doesn't matter how reasonable you are at this point, the narcissist is set on making a dramatic exit. Partners who aren't yet accustomed to the cycle will find this stage very heartbreaking as they may think they are losing the narcissist for good.

- **STAGE FOUR - The Return**

If you give the narcissist an opening, they'll come crawling back. Once they're done stirring up drama, the narcissist will try and pretend that they never did or said anything terrible. They'll hope that you, too, will try to let it slide. If you forgive them and allow them to get away with what they did, you'll start back over at stage one, where the narcissist will begin showering you in affection again. This final stage is crucial as it determines whether the cycle continues or if it finally gets better from here. It is at this point that the enabler of the narcissist should think about setting down some real rules.

Now that we've established the four stages of the narcissist cycle, we can finally work on the essential lessons all enablers must learn.

1. Understand that You're in Charge of Breaking the Cycle

Make no mistake, if you want to change the way this cycle plays out, it's up to you to take action and demand improvements. The narcissist will not make any changes on their own. They will continue on the same path because it has always worked for them. They do not have a high enough level of empathy to change on their own for the sake of your happiness. Their priority is getting what they want and they will believe this is the correct way until you show them it no longer works. The narcissist will not change – so you must.

2. Never Blame Yourself

Even though your demands are in charge of breaking the cycle, this doesn't mean you should blame yourself if it goes wrong. When your narcissist displays abusive behavior, it is never your fault. Hold them accountable for their decisions. As soon as you take the fall for something that is not your mistake, the narcissist will feel they have won. They will feel victorious in that moment and worse yet, this will encourage them to misbehave in the future. If they know you'll blame yourself and let them get off scot-free, they will continue down this upsetting path. If they made the choice, they alone should hold the blame.

3. Vow to Make Sure Every Violation is Punished

Always remember that narcissists just want to get their way. Teach them that abuse will only get them further away from their desire. Whenever they do or say anything hurtful, punish them by withdrawing from the situation. Before you do, let them know you are angry and that you will not cooperate in any way if they are resorting to abuse. Show them that as soon as abuse enters the conversation, you are not participating. Removal from the situation is usually the best course of action since some narcissists find pleasure in big displays of emotion. To them, this means you care and this emotion can be used against you. Even if the narcissist says something mildly insulting, they'll begin to learn that even this is unacceptable if you stop allowing them to get away with it.

4. Call Them Out on Everything

Using the narcissist cycle detailed above, keep an eye on which stage your narcissist is in at all times. Whenever you notice them making a power move or trying to manipulate the situation in any way, call them out on it. This is frustrating to the narcissist because they always think they're outsmarting the people around them. If you let them know you're aware of their tactics, this will show them their usual methods don't work. By pointing out their manipulative ways, you can corner them into being more honest with you.

5. Understand that Stage Two is Unavoidable

Unfortunately, there's no way to avoid the perceived betrayal when you're dealing with the narcissist. Unless, of course, you plan on letting them do whatever they want at all times. While you can't steer clear of their strong emotions, you can help them find better ways to express these emotions. Ideally, these improved ways should not involve any form of abuse. If the narcissist is having a bad day, then always do what you can to protect yourself from the fallout of stage two. If you're in a fragile place, you may want to get away for a while and turn your phone off. Or perhaps meditate before you decide to talk to them.

6. Implement Stronger Boundaries at Stage Four

The narcissist has some time to calm down at stage three, so by the time stage four rolls around, try and put down some stronger boundaries. This is the stage where the cycle ends and begins all over again. If you want to start with a healthier dynamic, make this clear to the narcissist once the big explosion has finally settled. It is at this point that the narcissist will be most likely to absorb what you're saying. If you're not sure what boundaries to set, consider the following questions: what was the trigger this time? What abusive or unhealthy responses did they display when they became upset? What did you feel most hurt by? Draw boundaries around their abusive behavior and discuss healthier ways they can let their grievances be known. Be clear about what behaviors you find unacceptable at stage two and be firm about how there will be consequences next time.

7. Know that Attachment or Addiction is Not the Same as Love

If you're in a relationship with an abusive narcissist, consider seeking professional help or leaving the situation, especially if you think your emotional well-being is at stake. Unless the narcissist is committed to improving their ways, it is highly unlikely that they'll make lasting changes for the better. Enablers often stay with their narcissist partners as they're convinced the narcissist will change if they just stick around a little longer. Unfortunately, this results in a lot of wasted time and even more hurt feelings. The enablers will always claim to have a deep love for the narcissist - and in some cases, this may be true - but more often than not, the narcissist just has them hooked. Intermittent reinforcement (the cycle of showing love, pulling it away, then giving it back) is scientifically proven to create feelings that mimic addiction. Often enablers are so hooked to the rollercoaster cycle of the narcissist that they mistake this attachment for love. It's extremely important that you make the distinction between these two different feelings.

The 10 Terrible Habits You Need to Quit Immediately

1. Asking Where Your Partner is at All Times

It's normal to have check-ins with your partner but many codependent people take this to a new level. Every hour to every couple of hours, the codependent couple will feel the need to ask the other partner where they are. What sets this behavior apart from the check-ins of non-codependent couples is the frequency with which they happen and the attitude behind them. When codependent couples check in with each other, there tends to be anxiety behind their questioning. They aren't just curious but they *need* to know. The next time you're apart from your partner, see if you can keep check-ins limited to once every four or five hours at the very least.

2. Looking Through Your Partner's Phone

A surprising number of people are guilty of snooping through their partner's phone. Having done it once or twice is not a big deal but it should *never* become a habit. If you need to look through your partner's devices to get peace of mind, your relationship needs a lot of work. If either partner is worried or anxious, the solution should always be to bring it up with your partner so you can cooperate on the basis of trust. If you can't do this, you should learn to let it go by developing the appropriate detachment tools. Snooping through someone's phone is a violation of privacy, no matter how discreet. A major step towards breaking codependency is learning to respect each other's personal space. Stop snooping!

3. Inviting Your Partner to Every Hangout with Friends

157

There's absolutely nothing wrong bringing your partner into your friend circle. In fact, some of the best times to be had are likely to come about when this happens. No matter how much fun it is, you should always make sure to get some alone time with your friends. To continue having happy and fulfilling friendships, the initial bond should be nurtured – and this doesn't involve your partner. Your friends may not tell you but they, too, wish they could have you alone sometimes. The dynamic changes once someone's significant other is in the room, and although this dynamic may still be fun, there's nothing like getting quality time the way it once used to be. A great way to maintain a healthy level of independence is by nurturing your relationships and friendships away from your partner, as well as with them.

4. Dropping Everything For Your Partner Immediately

There are times when it's perfectly acceptable to drop everything for your partner. If they're having an emergency, then absolutely go and help them – but don't abandon your life for anything less than this, except for rare occasions. If you're about to have a day of important meetings and your partner is feeling sad, wait till you're done with your obligations. Being sad is not an emergency. Your partner should be able to handle their emotions for a few hours. If you're planning on going to a friend's birthday party but your partner has a cold, do not cancel your original plans! When we get in the habit of abandoning our obligations for our partner, we send the message that nothing and no one else matters. This is a highly destructive attitude to take and one that will lead to a lot of regret in other areas of your life. Let professional and personal development be just as important as your partner.

5. Expecting Your Partner to Always Cheer You Up

We can't avoid feelings of sadness, frustration, or even depression. During these low points, our relationship can be a great source of relief and happiness. If your partner does something special for you in your moment of sadness, this should be considered a bonus, not a necessity.

Unless your partner made a mistake which they're apologizing for, it should never be the responsibility of your loved one to make you feel better. It is reasonable to expect that they treat is with consideration, but our inner turmoil is our own to deal with and no one else's responsibility. A major sign of codependency is the expectation that our partner's will fix everything for us. It's essential that you learn the necessary tools to deal with your issues privately. Your partner has his or her own issues to deal with.

6. Saying You're "Fine" When You're Anything But

If you're trying to quit codependency, you need to learn how to talk to your partner honestly. Stop sweeping everything under the rug. This doesn't mean there needs to be a huge blowout or a big deal made about everything; it just means you need to be honest if something bothers you. When we dismiss our feelings, we risk allowing problematic behavior to continue. Furthermore, we raise the possibility of building resentment or dissatisfaction in the long-term. Both of these outcomes with affect your relationship negatively. For a healthy and happy relationship, learn to talk about your feelings in a constructive and open way. A good rule of thumb is to communicate in "I feel" statements as opposed to accusations, i.e. you would say "I feel upset about what you said" instead of "What you said was upsetting."

7. Frequent Interrogations

Every time we interrogate our partners, we demonstrate that we do not entirely trust them. If you have trust issues due to past trauma, there's a way to seek reassurance from your partner without resorting to interrogations. Instead of firing a hundred emotionally charged questions at your partner, try stating that you feel insecure and need them to reassure you. This is a more honest approach to the situation and it is a far more kind way to behave. When we interrogate our partners, this creates anxiety in them whether they did anything wrong or not. Let's not forget that interrogations are meant to intimidate – to extract an answer by forcing someone into submission. If you want to have a healthy dynamic with your partner, leave out all intimidation or scare tactics. This will only make your partner afraid of you and it could backfire on your relationship. Learn to build stronger trust or find kinder ways of getting the response you need.

8. Stalking Your Partner Online

It's no secret that trust is essential to building a strong relationship. For the same reason you shouldn't snoop through your partner's phone or interrogate them, you should also resist the urge to stalk them online. People who do this will frequently check their partner's social media page, keeping up with their latest 'likes,' comments, and shares. This modern-day habit of keeping tabs on our partner can easily get obsessive and lead to suspicions or upsets over nothing. Many codependents will engage in this behavior without even thinking of the deeper implications. Quit the habit of monitoring your partner's behavior. Talk out your issues with them or learn to let go.

9. Making Every Social Media Post About Your Partner

There are many signifiers of codependence that are unique to modern day and this is one of them. If nearly every post on your social media involves your partner then this is a big sign that your identity is highly dependent on them. As we've established, an identity that revolves around another person is a key symptom of codependency. In a healthy relationship, one's sense of self should be clearly defined outside of the relationship. Interests, hobbies, opinions, likes, and dislikes should not be dependent on the other person in the relationship. If you're looking for an easy codependent habit to quit, try this one. Explore your social media presence without it being so closely linked to your relationship.

10. Helping Your Partner with Everyday Adult Tasks

This screams 'codependency' like few other bad habits. It's completely normal to help your partner out every once in a while, especially if you have a little free time, but do not make it a habit unless they're doing something similar for you in return. If you have extra time to make your partner a packed lunch, then sure, why not? Have you made a routine of packing lunch while your partner makes dinner every night? That sounds like a great balance of tasks. But if you're doing this everyday and not getting anything back, then this is straight-up codependent behavior. In all that you do, ensure that you never 'baby' your partner. Do not perform tasks that all other adults are doing for themselves. If you can do it for yourself, your partner can do it for him or herself too. It's time to let your partner be the grown-up they are.

Believe or not, destructive and dysfunctional behavior are not just about abuse. They can also consist of small, everyday habits that appear harmless at first glance. Over time, however, they wear away at trust and the bond underneath a relationship. To make room for growth, start eliminating these harmful compulsions.

Chapter 6: Detachment Strategies

Underneath every codependency is an unhealthy level of attachment. Partners have merged their identities into one, to the point where they no longer feel they have a separate identity outside of their relationship. What's ironic is that attachment is usually formed through an attempt to create a unique identity. However, we only get ourselves further from this goal since this new identity is so interwoven with somebody else.

Not all codependent partnerships will have outright destructive tendencies but the severe attachment is no less harmful to the individuals involved. In order to break the codependency, both partners must learn to find a healthy detachment from each other. Healthy detachment still allows for expectations and dependency, but removes the sense of desperation and helplessness. Codependent people tend to find this idea intimidating because they feel like codependence is synonymous with love – but once they break this dynamic, they instantly feel liberated. Love that stems from want instead of need is far more fulfilling for everyone involved. To discover what this feels like, make use of these detachment strategies for a more empowering dynamic.

9 Great Habits that Start Healing Codependency

You know all about the bad habits that need to be broken – now, it's time to tell you about the great habits that should replace them. Implement these new practices into your daily life to start seeing a healthy detachment from your partner. By absorbing these new ways into your relationship dynamics, you'll immediately start feeling less codependent.

1. Respond, Don't React

Due to past trauma, some of us have certain reactions wired into our brain. Without even thinking about it, we can find ourselves giving into these impulses out of pure habit. For example, if you were cheated on in the past, you may find it triggering if your current partner has a close friend of the opposite sex. Whenever your partner mentions seeing them, you may immediately feel betrayed and angry, even when you have no reason to be. A good rule of thumb to avoid unnecessary upsets is to cut the impulse off before it takes control. Instead of simply reacting out of habit, take the time to really listen to what your partner is saying. Consider if what they're saying is actually unreasonable or if you're just overcome by bad memories. Respond to what your partner is telling you in the here and now, instead of something that happened in the past.

2. Nurture Your Wants & Needs

Don't lose yourself in your relationship. If there are any interests or hobbies calling out to you, why not pique your curiosity? Dive into new curiosities and continue exploring your established interests. Stop suppressing your wants, needs, curiosities, likes, and dislikes. Nurture and encourage everything that makes you *you*. This will strengthen your sense of self, ensuring your identity is still entirely yours even when you're in an intimate relationship. Having different needs and desires isn't just good for the sake of it; it allows both partners separate worlds to escape into so that they can always remember what makes them unique. This way, they never lose their life purpose and stay firmly connected to their essence.

3. Make Personal Space Non-Negotiable

Don't just *try* to get personal space sometimes; you need to make personal space a non-negotiable. Set aside a day or time when you get to have space to do whatever you want – and of course, without your partner. Stop seeing personal space as a daunting idea and start to recognize it as absolutely essential for maintaining your happiness in the long run. See it as a must-have. Even if you think you'll miss your partner, that's no reason to cling and never let go. Why wait till you're sick of them before you have personal space? Missing someone we get to be with later is an incredible joy. It means the love and excitement is still alive. By making personal space a core part of your lifestyle, you'll ensure that this love and excitement stays alive and doesn't fizzle out. Do whatever you enjoy and give each other space to breathe. This does wonders for every relationship.

4. Be Accountable for Your Actions

As soon as you do this, you create an atmosphere of honesty, humility, and courage within the relationship. Being accountable for our actions and admitting when we've made a mistake can be difficult – but it shouldn't be. When we avoid accountability, we are essentially trying to say we are powerless and everything just happens to us – that it's not our fault because we have no influence over the situation. Why is this a good thing? When we're powerless we cannot take action to make things better. We become slaves to circumstance and the whims of other people. This is why being accountable is so transformative. You are recognizing your influence and control, and by doing so, you are also recognizing your capabilities of making things better. When one partner gets into the habit of taking accountability and owning up to their failures, the other partner (provided they are not a narcissist) begins to get comfortable doing the same. A couple that becomes accountable for their separate actions is a strong couple. There is significantly less upset and frustration in the relationship. Instead of needless blame and sour emotions, there can finally be a focus on solutions. The next time you make a mistake, tell your partner you realized what you did, that you're sorry, and you want to improve things next time. Do not play the blame game.

5. Call Out Your Partner for their Unhealthy Behavior

Just as you should be accountable for your actions, so should your partner. Sometimes it's not easy to recognize when we've made a mistake, especially when certain behaviors are routine. In this case, it's very important for the other partner to gently draw it to their attention. If they don't know, how can they improve themselves for the future? If you notice your partner displaying behavior that is unhealthy or even self-destructive, get into the habit of letting them know immediately. It's also essential that you do this constructively and with kindness. If you are angry and abusive, it is likely that they will respond negatively, adding further hindrances to the relationship's evolution. If your partner starts to guilt-trip you for wanting to spend time with your friends, address this codependent behavior. Say, "Honey, I felt like you were trying to guilt-trip me for seeing my friends and it worries me that we're resorting back to our codependent ways. How can we fix this for next time? I'd love it if we could find a solution so I can get some quality time with my friends. It's important to me that I see them sometimes." See, that's not so hard, is it?

6. Determine Your Personal and Professional Goals

Maintain a strong sense of self by continuing to grow and evolve. If you find yourself feeling stagnant or as though your relationship has consumed you, take time to sit down and reflect. Oftentimes we can lose direction because we haven't identified our wants and our goals. Think about what you'd like to accomplish in the near and distant future, then break these goals down into achievable steps. These can be professional goals, personal goals, or both. Is there a skill you'd like to take further? A new milestone you'd like to achieve? Would you like to lose or gain weight? Is there an artistic masterpiece you'd like to complete or at least get started on? There are numerous goals you can set for your life. Choose something that ignites excitement and joy in you. When we establish goals for ourselves, it becomes much easier to avoid codependency since we are instinctively trying to meet our own goals. It gives us something to strive for that is entirely about our own life and not directly connected to our partner. Make sure you always goals you're trying to meet, even if they are small goals.

7. Get an Outside Opinion

In the most extreme codependencies, both partners shy away from speaking to other people about their issues, especially those pertaining to their relationship. They have developed such an intense closeness to their partner that they feel they don't need anyone else. Unfortunately, this also means that when legitimate issues or problems arise in the relationship, they don't have anyone to tell. An outsider's perspective can be hugely beneficial, especially when it comes from a close friend or family member. Make sure neither you nor your partner shut out your respective support networks. They'll be able to tell when your codependency is getting too damaging. Learn to see this as helpful feedback and not just something inconvenient you'd rather not hear. When we're too close to a situation, it can be difficult to see everything as it is. Rely on your friends and family to tell you what you need to hear. Get in the habit of reaching out and maintaining your outside connections.

8. Say 'No' More Often

There's a huge misconception that if we love someone, we should let them do whatever they want. Hopefully by now, you've realized this could not be more wrong. Never saying 'no' to your partner is one of the key things that can lead to codependency. It essentially means you have no boundaries for your partner. When you get in the habit of saying 'no' to your partner, you're standing up for your needs and desires, conveying that they are just as important as your partner's. It is not cruel to say 'no' as oftentimes 'doormat' tendencies can lead to a quiet resentment in codependent partners. By setting boundaries, you're ensuring that you never exhaust yourself by giving more than you have. Down the road, this means you'll be happier, more fulfilled, and far more ready to be a good partner. The kindness you show your loved one will be born out of genuine love instead of necessity and obligation.

9. Solve Problems Together

When someone in a relationship makes a mistake, people tend to oversimplify the solution-finding process. They tend to think, "You made the mistake, so you should fix it. Figure it out and get back to me when things are better." We leave the person who made the mistake to come up with a solution on their own. Many couples believe this is the fair thing to do, but it's far from it. Healthy couples solve problems together. This does not mean both partners are at fault. It shows they recognize two heads are better than one. If you truly want to fix the situation and not just 'get even,' you should work alongside your partner to find a solution. Examine the problem at hand, what went wrong, and what could be better next time. Get in the habit of cooperating instead of making just one partner responsible for change.

4 Unique Challenges to Get Used to Healthy Detachment

If you're extremely codependent, the thought of detachment may sound scary to you. To simplify your next few steps, consider experimenting with the following challenges. These will help you get in the proper mindset for finding your own independence. At the end of each challenge, reunite with your partner and share your different experiences. See if you can have some fun with these challenges!

1. Draw Your Day

You don't need to have an artistic streak for this challenge – in fact, it might be more fun if you don't! For this challenge, both partners should separate for several hours and draw what they see, wherever they choose to go. They can take their pick of anything they see that day – it can be funny, serious, or even surrealist, if they so desire! Ideally, both partners shouldn't text each other except to discuss logistics about where and what time to meet up later. At the end of the day, both partners can reunite and show each other what they drew. If you're a terrible artist, laughing at your bad drawings could make for a hilarious evening. This challenge is one of the best since it allows people to get in touch with their creative side while also getting personal space. And the benefits don't end there! Partners always enjoy looking over each other's drawings and sharing the stories connected to what they saw.

2. Meet in the Middle

If there's an adventurous side to you, try the 'Meet in the Middle' challenge with your partner. Put simply: it requires both partners to explore two opposite or faraway locations and then meet up again halfway. This challenge can be scaled to suit your time frame and budget. If you're not able to travel internationally, there's no need to fret! Each partner can choose a city or town in the country that they've always wanted to explore. This works especially well if the other partner has already been there or doesn't care to go. Once both people have chosen their city or town, they can pinpoint a location that's roughly halfway. After traveling through and exploring separate locations, they can make their way to each other and meet in that halfway spot. If you have a bigger budget, consider doing this with countries. Solo travel is an empowering experience and couples, inevitably, find the 'halfway meetup' to be incredibly romantic.

3. The Gift Exchange

Just like 'Draw Your Day,' this challenge involves a couple separating for a few to several hours. There should be no communication whatsoever until it's time to reunite, later on in the day. The goal of their time apart should be to purchase, create, or just somehow procure a gift for their partner. The target can be one gift or more, depending on their respective budgets. It would also be wise for both partners to decide on a spending limit, so one person doesn't outspend the other. This is a great challenge to start off with since both partners can still feel close to each other in the pursuit of a gift for their loved one.

4. Outside-Inside

No excuses allowed for this one! One person is in charge of 'Outside' and the other is in charge of 'Inside.' For as long as it takes to finish, both partners must focus on their separate tasks without help from the other. Partners can only communicate over logistics or if they're asking for clarification. All other communication must be saved for after the challenge, when everything is complete. Here's a rundown of what each person is in charge of:

Outside - All errands that involve going out such as grocery shopping, sending mail, picking up tools or materials for repairs, refilling the car with gas, depositing a check or withdrawing money for rent, and many others. It can also include household chores if they take place outside, e.g. gardening, yard work, shed repairs, etc.

Inside - All duties regarding the inside of the home and general housekeeping. This includes doing laundry, making beds, cleaning and dusting the home, tidying and reorganizing clutter, doing dishes, and all other home-related chores.

Whoever finishes first gets to have free time to do whatever they want! The only condition? They must stay away from their partner until all chores are completed.

Why not create your own challenge? For the best outcome, both partners should be separated for as long as possible while focusing on a clearly defined goal or enjoying a distraction.

Chapter 7: Personal Space & Self-Care

We've spoken a lot about personal space and self-care, but some of you may be wondering, "What exactly does that entail?" or "What do I do once I have personal space?" If you're at the extreme end of codependent, you may need some ideas for your next self-care sesh. As we've established, this is crucial for maintaining a healthy level of independence in your relationship. When partners continue to practice this in a relationship, they become stronger, more courageous individuals that see more life fulfillment in the long run. If you're intimidated by the thought of having temporary separation, understand that it's only difficult for one reason: you're breaking a fixed routine! It's in no way indicative of the effects it will ultimately have. Destructive or not, patterns are difficult to break – but once you succeed, your life blossoms in ways you could never have imagined.

6 Reasons Why Personal Space Heals Couples

Before you can come up with excuses for skipping the rest of this chapter, let's examine the benefits of personal space. On the days you're overwhelmed by anxiety, when you just want to cling and never let go, turn back to this section. This is why personal space is vital for healing codependency:

1. It Makes You a Stronger Person

When we are given space to do our own thing, we use coping and self-management tools that we stop using in the presence of our close loved ones. If we have a need, we learn to take care of it on our own. We learn to provide our own entertainment. And we can finally listen and assess our own thoughts, without influence from an outside party. That pang you feel when you're by yourself and you really wish someone was there with you – that's your mind refusing to use your own self-management tools. When we have someone around us, we don't have to use them as much. They can help us perform tasks, entertain us, and they provide us with as many distractions as we desire. This feels good

170

in the same way sitting on the couch, instead of going to work, feels good. It allows us to not do any work, but it damages our ability to fend for ourselves and be self-sufficient. If you don't learn to be strong now, it'll be a hundred times more difficult in the future. Personal space gives us the opportunity to self-manage again and this brings a lot of benefits with it.

2. Reconnecting to Our Individuality Makes Us Happier

When we get personal space, we our reminded of what makes us different. Instead of merging with our partner's identity, we remember our own and what exactly makes us unique. When we reconnect with this part of ourselves, we instantly feel happier. Why? It's simple. We all want to feel special. No one wants to feel like they've become exactly like something else. Those who do are under the mistaken impression that merging identities is the cure to not feeling special. This, of course, could not be further from the truth. To truly feel one-of-a-kind and unique, we need to connect to something deep in ourselves. This part of us can only be accessed through sufficient time alone. As much as you love your partner, too much time together can make you forget what makes you different.

3. There's More to Talk About Later On

If you're always with each other, you're receiving the same general experience at the same time. This can be special too, of course; you can discuss events as they unfold around you and enjoy sharing in the same experience. But don't forget, there's also enjoyment to be had in having different experiences and telling the story later on. Two partners that reunite after a long day apart can relay the stories and events of the day to one another, relishing the storytelling and the surprise element that comes with it. When we're always with our partner, we miss out on the fun of catching up.

4. You Can Get Sick of Great Things, Too – Don't Let This Happen!

You may love and cherish your partner deeply. You may even think your relationship is the best thing in the world and you're so meant for each other that nothing can ruin what you have. I hate to break it to you: too much time together can, indeed, ruin it. Let's say you discovered the world's best pancakes. You found them so delicious you decided to have them for every meal. At first, having your favorite food three times a day seemed like heaven – but what about after a few months? Or a few years? You'd definitely start to get sick of it. Eventually, you'd start to crave literally *anything* else. It doesn't matter how objectively good those pancakes are or how much you enjoyed them in the beginning. If you overdo it, you won't want anything more to do with them. The same goes for you and your partner. Without personal space, the relationship starts to feel suffocating. This will inevitably lead to a more strained partnership.

5. It Reminds You of Why You're Together

When we are constantly with someone or something that we love, we start to take them for granted. We get so accustomed to quick and easy access that we forget how special it is to have access at all. Couples that make personal space a part of their lifestyle experience a lot more gratitude towards their partner. When they're together, they're reminded of the joy that their significant other brings to their life. The periods of being apart create a contrast against the times they are together. This immediately highlights the positive differences their relationship makes. In turn, this makes every moment together seem more special. Partners will appreciate each other much more and be happier in the long run.

6. Happier People Create More Lasting Relationships

Codependence is formed when couples are too anxious or insecure to let each other go. Ironically, learning to do so can actually make the chances of staying together (happily) more likely. Consider everything we've covered so far. There will be more excitement, you won't get sick of each other, *you'll* be happier and so will your partner. Two happy, strong individuals make a happy, strong couple. To ensure lasting satisfaction, there needs to be room to grow. By giving each other space, you're allowing each other space to evolve into better selves. Couples that do this thrive better than the rest.

10 Ways to Accelerate Self-Growth While You Have Personal Space

Codependent people struggle to fill their time when they finally have personal space. Many begin to feel anxiety, not sure what to do with themselves now that their partner isn't there. It's helpful to note this only happens because it is a break from their usual routine. It can be overcome with practice. Personal space is a great time to finally focus on self-growth and make strides towards accomplishing your personal goals. Making the effort to always keep your goals in sight will help you ward off your codependent leanings. Consider the many ways you can do this:

1. Learn a New Skill

Is there a talent you secretly wish you had? When was the last time you thought 'I wish I could do that'? A workshop or class is a fantastic thing to add to a schedule and it's a great use of personal time. It can be anything from painting and photography classes to kung fu lessons. The sky's the limit when it comes to learning. You could even choose to improve a skill that leads to a higher income down the road. Perfecting a new skill will remind you of your worth and capabilities beyond your relationship. Have fun with this one. The world is your oyster!

2. Go to the Gym

Make gym sessions part of your weekly routine and you'll see benefits beyond just your appearance. Not only will you look fitter and more toned, but most importantly, you'll *feel* stronger. And you'll instantly see a boost in your level of self-esteem and confidence. Working out is a great way to prove to yourself that you can overcome adversity –

this determination and strength will extend beyond your time at the gym, improving your relationship and likely even your professional confidence. Take care of your body and your entire mindset will reflect this positive transformation.

3. See a Therapist

It's time to remove the stigma around therapy! You don't need a mental health condition in order to see a therapist. Having a session once a week or every couple of weeks is a great way to destress and declutter the mind. Getting restless emotions and thoughts out of the way gives you more time to focus on what really matters. Therapy can be especially beneficial for people in a codependent relationship. A neutral figure will be able to point out when codependent habits are surfacing and help you evolve out of them. They can help you tackle the root cause of your issues so you never again have to call yourself 'codependent.'

4. Experiment with Cooking Healthier Meals

We all know how to cook *something* in the kitchen, but how many delicious, truly healthy meals can you cook? In your spare time, why not experiment in the kitchen with some body-nourishing foods. When we focus our attention on feeding ourselves, our minds find a calm center. Why? Because we are going back to basics and doing something that literally keeps us alive. We are giving attention to the fundamentals of our being and this can be meditative. Try and cook with new ingredients, have fun with new flavors, and see what delicious creations you can come up with.

5. Plan Your Future and Set Goals

Now that you have some alone time, why not see if you can define your goals for the near and distant future? What would you like to accomplish? Where would you like to go? What are some habits you'd like to break and some better habits you'd like to pick up? While you're doing this, try and make your first draft of goals without considering what your partner (or anyone else) would say about them. Just focus on your goals and dreams. Once you clearly identify what these are, weight out how important each one is to you. How happy will you be if you achieve each one? Will the inability to achieve a certain goal lead to unhappiness? Answer these questions before thinking of what your partner would say. Consider making the goals that would make you deeply happy a non-negotiable.

6. Read a Good Book

They say the world's most successful entrepreneurs read dozens of books a year. It's no wonder why. Not only is reading entertaining, but it can broaden your horizons in ways that change your perspective and outlook for the better. Whether it's fiction or nonfiction, reading brings many benefits including memory improvement and stress reduction. Over time, you'll find your vocabulary expanding and it may even enhance your writing skills. Incorporate more reading time into your schedule (now that you have more peace and quiet!) and you'll supercharge that mind of yours in no time.

7. Start a Creative Project

You don't need to be an artistic genius to start a creative project. It's as simple as choosing a medium you enjoy and having fun with it. Encouraging your own creativity helps you destress and in the long run, improves your problem-solving abilities. Studies have even shown that creativity enhances one's ability to adapt to new changes. The next time you have time to yourself, why not try painting or sketching? Or pick up an instrument and learn to sing?

8. Learn to Develop a Growth Mindset

As you pursue new hobbies and skills in your spare time, try and develop a growth mindset. A fixed mindset is driven by the belief that everyone is born with certain talents and gifts, and all those who are not 'gifted' will never achieve the same level of brilliance. The growth mindset comes as a firm opposition to this, asserting that we can indeed reach the same level of brilliance if we persist and continue improving ourselves. While you have personal space, try to absorb this growth mindset into your mental space. Not only will this help you improve certain skills, it will also help you grow out of your codependency. You don't have to be codependent forever; a growth mindset will ensure you leave your old habits behind for good.

9. Take Breaks from Tech

While you're taking a break from your partner, why not take a Break with a capital B from all the chaos of the modern world? You can choose whatever timeframe you're most comfortable with – but it should pose a little bit of a challenge! For at least a couple of hours, turn off all your communication and entertainment devices. Completely disconnect from all digital distractions and do not communicate with your partner in any way during this time. Feel free to do whatever you like during this time as long as you are in charge of creating your own entertainment (do not go to a bar and watch their TV!) and you're allowing yourself to be alone with your thoughts. Practicing No Tech time can decrease anxiety over time as you begin to get used to silence and temporary disconnection.

10. Have a Conversation with a Stranger

This may seem like an odd suggestion, but learning to be comfortable around strangers has a number of different benefits. Not only do you improve your social skills, but you learn to become adaptable to different situations and different personalities. You also have no idea who you might meet! There are connections just waiting to be made all around you. Expanding your circle of friends is a great way to ensure you don't rely too heavily on your partner.

12 Self-Care Ideas to Make You Feel Like a Million Bucks

Of course, personal space should also be about self-care. When codependents are completely wrapped up in each other, they forget to take care of their own self. Often we don't realize how much we need self-care until we finally experience it. The result: we're calm, centered, and at peace in every single way. This puts is in a better mood, making us more pleasant individuals. In turn, this makes us better partners.

There's no need to reserve self-care for when we're completely alone. Self-care should be part of your routine and you can do it by yourself or with your partner close by. That's up to you. However you choose to care for yourself, make sure you always make time for it so it can be a consistent part of your life.

1. Bubble Baths

You've probably seen it happen in movies. During times of relaxation, a character is neck deep in a bubble bath surrounded by candles. Why not try it in real life? Bubbles or no bubbles, candles or bathroom lights, music or silence: the choice is yours. Discover what kind of environment helps you achieve a deep calm and try to get to that quiet place in your mind. Forget the world for a moment and relax.

2. Massage

Getting a massage requires no effort from you. Just find a spa or masseuse that you like the sound of, and enjoy being pampered. A massage session makes brilliant self-care because the kneading opens up the body and – of course – it just *feels* amazing. The gentle pressure all over the body relieves stress by releasing dopamine, reducing anxiety and instantly making you feel more calm, no matter what. It doesn't need to be complicated; just lay down and allow yourself to feel good.

3. Coffee and a Good Book

Since the dawn of hipster cafes, the coffee-and-a-book routine has become a brilliant modern way of achieving self-care. Get out of your space and spend a few hours in a coffee shop. Order a steaming cup of coffee or a creamy hot chocolate, find your spot, and finally delve into that great book you've heard so much about. Believe it or not, just getting out of your personal space can reduce anxiety. The coffee-and-a-book routine allows you to simplify your life for just a moment. All you have to do is enjoy your comfy spot, focus on your book, whilst nourishing your belly with warm, rich goodness.

4. Go Shopping

Let's preface this by saying: don't go overboard! Know what your budget and stick to it. And other than that? Have fun and treat yourself to whatever makes you feel good. There's a reason the term 'retail therapy' exists. When we shop, we get to indulge our wants and needs. This is good practice for the codependent who tends to be focused on other people's wants and needs. Take this moment to shut your codependent brain out and consider what purchase would excite you in the here and now.

5. Get a Makeover

Sometimes there's no better way to feel good than by making yourself *look* good. There are no rules to getting a makeover – just have fun experimenting with your appearance with the goal of making yourself feel attractive. If you're female, consider purchasing the services of a makeup artist. Both genders can enjoy getting a few different outfits for their wardrobe or freshening up with a new haircut. The possibilities are endless!

6. Talk to Friends

Talking and laughing with friends is its own form of therapy. While you're engaging in self-care, why not have a catch up session with some of your most trusted friends? Not only does this provide stress relief but it's been proven that spending time with friends leads to a longer lifetime and improved mental health. Whether you decide to indulge at a great restaurant or have a fun night in watching Netflix or a game, make sure that time with friends is a regular session in your schedule.

7. Write in a Journal

Journaling is great for codependent couples because it allows you to get in touch with your feelings. To keep the peace, codependents are known to shut their thoughts and feelings out – something that does not bode well for the health of the relationship. Journaling can help you declutter your mind and destress, allowing you to organize your thoughts and observe your inner world. Many people choose to write in their journals in the early morning or right before bedtime, as a way of calming the mind for the day or for restful sleep.

8. Meditate

When looking for the best self-care methods, meditation is suggested so often that it tends to elicit a roll of the eyes. There's a good reason why meditation is raved about; it has real, lasting benefits that genuinely make a difference to your mental well-being and life. To meditate successfully, one must try to clear their mind of all thoughts and simply be in the moment. To get started, try and focus your breath, and nothing else. Ideally, this should be done in a quiet space where one can sit down without being disturbed. Make meditation part of your self-care routine and you'll soon see reduced stress and anxiety, and an enhanced self-awareness and attention span.

9. Go For a Drive or Walk

This self-care method requires nothing but energy and time. Choose any starting point at all and just take a walk or drive from there onwards with no destination in sight. Just explore and keep going forwards. The purpose of this drive is to clear your mind and to have time alone with yourself, while still experiencing the motion of moving forwards. Going for a walk or drive is known to be emotionally healing; it allows you to be in full control of your path and destination, just going wherever you please and letting your thoughts find peace.

10. Redecorate

A fun way to achieve self-care is by redecorating your space. This could be anywhere you like. It could be your desk at work, your bedroom, or even your entire house. Redecorating can be incredibly fun as it allows us to use the creative side of our brain – but more than this, it is also an act of reclaiming our space and practicing our control over our surroundings. Make aesthetically pleasing choices and see if you can rearrange your belongings for the most convenience possible. Organize and decorate your space so that it becomes your own personal sanctuary. By the end, you should feel comfortable, relaxed, and inspired in your newly decorated space.

11. Exercise

Exercise isn't just a way to see more self-growth, it's also a great way to engage in self-care. It's only important that you don't overdo it and exhaust yourself. Whether it's a leisurely walk through the park or an intense session of pilates, exercise ensures that your body stays strong and capable. Many people think that exercise is so hard it can't possibly be self-care, but this is just a sign that you need it more than ever. Exercising allows us to reconnect with our vessel and to be more in tune with its needs and abilities. The rush of endorphins also means you'll instantly feel more positive about yourself and life in general.

12. Practice Gratitude

Believe it or not, it's been proven that practicing gratitude makes a person more happy. By training the brain to notice and be thankful for the positive things in life, we instantly begin to operate from a mindset of abundance. This improves our sense of self-esteem, our ability to empathize, and it even improves our quality of sleep. To begin practicing gratitude, find a place where you can begin making notes about what you're grateful for. This can be a special gratitude journal or it can be on the Notes app on your phone. Every day list down three things that you're grateful for in your life. Try and be as specific as possible. Remember that these don't have to be grand parts of your life, it can be as simple as the fantastic lunch you had or a great workout session. Just make sure whatever it is, you feel genuinely grateful for it.

Do not feel daunted by the idea of personal space. It's a chance for you to recalibrate, reenergize, and do what you need to do to sustain your own inner strength. It's a time to reconnect with the activities you enjoy and the purpose of your life. Learn not to see it as separation from your partner, but instead as powerful fuel for a healthy relationship.

Chapter 8: Healing Codependency For Good

A short message from the Author:

Hey! We've made it to the final chapter of the audiobook and I hope you've enjoyed it so far.

If you have not done so yet, I would be incredibly thankful if you could take just a minute to leave a quick review on Audible, even if it's just a sentence or two!

Many readers and listeners don't know how hard reviews actually are to come by, and how much they help an author.

To do so, just click the 3 dots in the top right corner of your screen inside of your Audible app and hit the "Rate and Review" button.

Then you'll be taken to the "rate and review" page where you can enter your star rating and then write a sentence or two.

It's that simple!

I look forward to reading your review as I personally read every single one.

I am very appreciative as your review truly makes a difference for me.

Now back to your scheduled programming.

We've broken down personalities of codependent partners, highlighted the habits that need to be eradicated, as well as the habits you need to start bringing into your life – but that's not all you need moving forward. The urges that lead to codependency run deep. Underneath the little habits and practices are some key and highly essential lessons. The smaller practices will certainly help in building a healthier day-to-day dynamic, but without absorbing these core lessons, you may find yourself relapsing back to square one. During particularly trying periods, feel free to return back to this chapter to remind yourself of what's important.

The Lessons that Break Codependency

- **'Tough Love' is Necessary – Embrace It**

Don't shy away from the notion of tough love. Simply put, tough love is when we give our loved ones certain boundaries or constraints with the intention of helping them grow in the long run. Even if they don't realize it, tough love is for *their* benefit. To heal codependency for good, you need to start embracing practices of tough love. This means saying no and setting limits even when you feel sorry for them and want to say yes. Codependents may struggle with guilt at first so it's important that you make a mindset shift during these moments. Instead of focusing on their reaction in the current moment, think of the benefits they'll see down the road. Think of the life-altering lessons this will teach them and how life will reward them for it if they persist. Do not be swayed by the temporary discomfort and focus all your attention on the potential growth of the situation. Tough love is a different kind of loving behavior, but it is loving no less.

- **Needs are Tools, not Enemies**

In codependent relationships, the enabler tends to see their needs as obstacles. After all, how can they take care of their partners needs when their own are getting in the way? For enablers to continue breaking their codependent patterns, they need to stop seeing their needs as inconveniences. Our wants and needs are tools. They tell us about our state of mind and what we need in our life to find satisfaction. Our needs give us the direction we desire. It tells us what we need for growth and what you need to sustain yourself emotionally and psychologically. Needs are, indeed, tools and indicators of growth. Do not shun them away or the urges will only become stronger. We become unhappy when we ignore these urges and try to suppress them. A need signifies a lack and if left unchecked, this can lead to a kind of emotional or mental depletion. Your needs are akin to the red light that goes on when your car starts to need more gas. These lights do you a favor by letting you know when they need something to keep going as normal. Treat your needs the same way. Do not let those red lights start flashing!

- **Nothing Changes if You Don't Change**

By now you've probably been faced with some harsh truths about your behavior and relationship. It's profoundly important that you don't stop here. The knowledge that you need to change is not enough in itself to create change. You feel unsatisfied, unfulfilled, like your relationship could be much better, and you're right – now do something about it. Use feelings of dissatisfaction as fuel to start taking action. Your codependency will not heal if you don't begin working with your partner to find a healthier dynamic. If you find yourself reverting back to your old ways, expect to revert back to your old feelings of frustration. If you want better for your relationship, *be* better.

- **Clinginess and Obsession are Not the Same as Love**

When you're completely wrapped up in your partner, it can be easy to think this obsession is equivalent to love. There's a big misconception that giving until you have nothing left and merging your identity with your partner is what true love means, but this only results in codependency. Moving forward, try to shift your perspective on what love means. Remember that love isn't just about how you are as a single unit, it's also about how the relationship affects you as an

184

individual. Does the relationship empower you to achieve your own dreams and goals? Or does it make you feel like giving up on the rest of your life? Does the relationship remind you of who you really are? Or does it completely eradicate your unique identity? Think of love in terms of the long-term future that you're building with your partner, not just about how instantly gratifying is. Try and understand that love doesn't take over our life; it helps the rest of our life to blossom. The more you cling to your partner, the less time and space there is for the rest of your life. Real love is about two whole people who come together in their full power, not two halves trying desperately to make a whole.

- **Stop Feeling Defeated by Rejection**

There's a reason why both partners fuel this cycle of codependency; they're afraid of what would happen if they stopped. The enabler is worried, on some level, about not being useful and the enabled partner is worried about being forgotten. Although both partners have different ways of coping, they're both trying to ensure they remain loved by the other partner. Why? Because the thought of losing their codependent partner is far too painful. Unfortunately, this type of mentality can backfire. When we are driven to act a certain way out of deep insecurity around loss and rejection, it can become a self-fulfilling prophecy. As difficult as it seems, both partners need to learn to be okay with the possibility of not being in their codependent relationship. In other words, they need to get comfortable with the idea of being single. When they think of losing their partner, it's normal to feel deep sadness but they shouldn't feel like their world will end. Getting comfortable with the idea doesn't mean you want it to happen – it simply means that if it's right, you'll accept it. At the end of the day, rejection lets us know what's right for us and what isn't. Instead of trying to avoid rejection from your partner at all costs, learn to see it as a way to measure your compatibility. If you're rejected after trying your best, then it wasn't meant for you. One day you'll discover what *is* meant for you and you'll be fine.

What to Do If...?

You're trying to break a codependency and that's a big deal. Many scenarios will arise that leave you feeling confused and unsure of what the 'right' thing to do is for the health of your relationship. The next time you find yourself 'stuck,' turn back to this page. When you find yourself faced with any of these scenarios, this is what you should do:

- **Your partner is not listening to your boundaries**

By the time you finish this book, you'll likely feel motivated to strive for a healthier relationship. Unfortunately, you can't control how your partner feels. It's possible he or she isn't quite ready to make new changes. One of the ways they'll make this known is by refusing to abide by your newly set boundaries. If you make an agreement to split up chores, you may find that your partner still doesn't do their fair share, leaving you with most of the work.

Before you determine the best way to respond, answer these questions: how many times have you had to remind your partner of the boundaries? How many strikes have there been? How disrespected do you feel? Your intuition is a strong way to measure this situation. If you feel like your partner is trying their best but they're just struggling to let go of old habits, then be firm with them. Don't shy away from showing them you're angry or upset. Make it clear that this means a lot to you. If you feel disrespected and like your partner genuinely isn't trying, then reconsider your involvement in this relationship. You're trying your best and it's only fair your partner tries too. You're ready for a better relationship and as long as your partner is stuck in their old ways, they'll hold you back from growth too. You deserve better.

- **Your partner is exaggerating their ailments as a way of rebelling against your new boundaries**

You've tried to set boundaries with your partner and they've responded by exaggerating their condition. They are doing everything they can to make sure they appear more helpless. Hopefully, you know why by now. They want to keep the cycle going. They are likely afraid and nervous about the new turn your relationship is taking and they want you to start behaving like your old self.

Remember that your partner has been taught to equate enabling with love. This change of behavior is probably making them feel insecure, wondering how they'll continue getting love from you if you no longer feel the need to help them. Try and point out this behavior, gently. Draw what they are doing to their attention and explain why they are behaving this way. They may not even realize it and may be reacting purely out of insecurity. After this, continue to be firm with your boundaries but make an extra effort to show them love in ways that do not encourage codependence. If they enjoy receiving gifts, give them flowers or anything that encourages a new hobby – but all the while, do not back down on making them do their chores. Replace codependent behavior with other loving behavior.

- **Your partner is suspicious of you whenever you have personal space**

Since you and your partner are so used to spending a lot of time together, it can be jarring once you finally add personal space to your daily lives. As a way to cope, your partner may even become suspicious, believing that your behavior is caused by a more malicious ulterior motive. After all, they're used to seeing love as synonymous with time together. It will take time to adjust to this new perspective and it may result in resistance. They may even fire off a few accusations. For example, they may believe that the real reason you want space is to make time for cheating or because you're trying to break up with them in a kind way. These are some of the many accusations that enablers may hear.

See this behavior for what it is. Your partner has been taught that love means clinging to each other so naturally they think the reverse means you don't care about them. Obviously this isn't true, so take the time to gently reassure them. Remind them that the reason you're trying to change is because you want to ensure your relationship succeeds. Personal space is a way to make sure your relationship is healthy and secure, not desperate and clingy. Come up with ways you can reassure your partner without resorting to codependent behavior. Similar to the previous scenario, show them love in new ways, such as buying them a gift every now and then or writing them a heartfelt card.

- **Your partner still can't take care of him or herself, even though you've given them space**

As we've established, overhelping takes away autonomy and empowerment. To help your partner reconnect with their inner strength, you've likely given them space to learn how to take care of their own needs. This is a positive move, on your part. However, you may find that your partner is still unable to help themselves. They're trying but they're failing. They're incompetent, getting things wrong all the time, and overall, not doing as good of a job as you used to do.

In these moments, it'll be tempting to revert back to your old behavior. Watching them fail will make you want to help them again. If they're truly struggling, it's alright to give them a little bit of assistance, but other than this, try to stay firm. Otherwise, you may find yourself regressing. They're struggling because this is new to them. You've had your whole life to learn how to do it the right way, but they're only learning now. It will take some time. Expect it to take some time. Be gentle with them and do what you can to support them as they learn, but do not do the work for them. If your partner has trouble making their own food, buy them a new cookbook or pay for a cooking lesson or two – but do not give in and start making all their lunches for them again! Have patience and do what you can to foster growth.

- **You've started to feel utterly useless and worthless**

Until now, you've gotten by as the 'fixer' in your relationship. You got accustomed to helping your partner with every little thing and easing their pain whenever you could. But let's not forget, it's not just about what your partner receives from you; your satisfaction comes in the form of feeling needed. When you know you're helping your partner, you feel useful. You feel like you're doing something that matters. Breaking out of codependent habits means you're trying not to overhelp and this new change has caused you to feel a little useless. This may even result in some depression.

Remind yourself that you *are* helping by stepping back. By doing this, you're allowing your partner to learn their lessons and achieve self-growth. Understand that when you're not in a codependent relationship, helping and being useful manifests in different behavior. You're accustomed to the codependent way of 'helping' – which is actually enabling. When we *really* help someone, we do what's best for them. And in this case, *not* overhelping is what's best for your partner. Recognize that what you're really craving is the instant gratification that comes from enabling your partner. By not forcing them to do anything, you're allowing them to do what pleases them in the moment. This may look like it's good for them, but in reality, it is the furthest thing from helping. Remember this distinction and resist the urge to overhelp at all costs.

This journey won't always be easy. In fact, at times you'll struggle and feel like it's too difficult to handle. Of course it's hard – after all, you're breaking response patterns that have been hardwired into your brain. What's important is that you recognize the hardship for what it is. It's growth. Keep these core lessons at the center of all your decisions and you'll soon be able to proudly say, "No, I'm not codependent."

Conclusion

Congratulations on completing *No More Codependency*! By making it to this page, you've taken great strides towards a more sustainable and healthy relationship dynamic. This is wonderful news – not just for you, but also for your partner. You've proven that you are truly committed to a happier future with your significant other and that you're willing to do what it takes to quit your codependent ways. You are so much closer to success than you think! If you need more motivation, all you have to do is turn back to this book. Everything you need is right here.

Hopefully, this book has empowered you to keep making these big, powerful strides. It's important you remember that codependent relationships are not a life sentence; relationship coaches and psychologists everywhere agree that codependencies can, indeed, be healed with time. By adhering to the helpful rules and tips in this book, you'll soon see your relationship in a whole new light. You'll be a happier, more fulfilled individual and your relationship will blossom in turn. What's important is that you continue to persist and remain self-aware.

We've covered the in-depth details of codependency, identifying what it really means and what exactly makes it different to everyday dependence on our loved ones. It's important that you recognize this distinction as there's no need to eliminate all of your dependent behavior – some of it is perfectly normal. By now, you're well aware of the difference between the two. Codependent behavior doesn't mean never depending on our partner. It simply means having a healthy level of dependence and knowing who you are without your partner.

Before you move forward, it's essential that you figure out which codependent partner you are. Are you the enabler or the enabled? Try to approach this question without any denial. We've covered the likely backgrounds of each partner and it's possible you saw yourself in those descriptions. Perhaps you were even able to pinpoint the exact relationship in your childhood that gave you this codependent mindset. Now that you've finished this book, try and work through those memories. Which early relationship taught you to be codependent? Delve deeply into yourself and recognize that this early relationship was likely very dysfunctional. Treating your relationship the same way will only result in the same dysfunctions. You don't want that, do you? Of course not.

Once you commit to change, you'll need to start laying down some boundaries. This means saying 'no' and setting some rules where necessary. It means conveying to your partner, in some way, that you'll no longer be fixing every little thing that goes wrong. Doing this can be difficult, especially since you're not used to it. You may even have feelings of guilt or uncertainty around how to enforce them. Pay close attention to the tips we've covered and you'll soon see boundaries as completely natural. You'll suddenly find yourself with far more energy, now that you're no longer exhausted from over-exerting and doing more than your fair share.

Aside from this, it's also important that you and your partner work on building your sense of self. This may mean developing stronger self-esteem and self-awareness. Using the affirmations and exercises in this book, you can begin rewiring your psyche to produce more positive thoughts about yourself. How can you make the most of your gifts and positive qualities if you never realize they exist? Whether you realize it or not, self-esteem is a big part of healing codependency. You need to recognize that you are enough and that you are wonderful, even without a partner at your side. By creating a more positive inner dialogue, you'll help your relationship thrive.

After learning about boundaries and developing self-esteem, you were faced with some big challenges. Namely, destructive behavior. Hopefully, you were motivated and inspired to finally eliminate these harmful habits from your life. You can't evolve if you don't get rid of the obstacles. Once you've identified what these obstacles are, you can work hard on moving past them. Now that you understand the cycle of narcissistic abuse, you can hopefully recover from any abuse you've endured. If you're staying in a relationship with a narcissist, hold on tight. It may be a turbulent ride. Turn back to the section on narcissistic abuse and do your best to enact the changes that were listed – otherwise, you may find yourself stuck in a cycle that never ends. Remember this: if you don't change, nothing will!

With new detachment strategies and exercises under your belt, you can finally discover independence. Allow this to feel liberating because it is. Have fun with the challenges and enjoy how it feels to finally have personal space. By now, you'll know all about the importance of personal time and space. The next time you find yourself lost about what to do with yourself, rest assured you've got a solid list of ideas for what to do. Consider engaging in an activity that promotes self-growth or refreshes you through self-care. You need both in equal measure!

The core lessons that are integral to healing codependency have been summed up into bite-sized pieces. Turn back to the final chapter, if you ever find yourself wavering. Remind yourself of these lessons and make sure that every change you make is fueled by them. If a difficult scenario arises with your partner, this chapter will also give you ideas for what to do. There's always a solution as long as both partners are committed to growth. Don't let 'enabler' and 'enabled' define your life together. Explore your individuality, learn healthy detachment, and shower your entire life (not just your relationship) in love. Show yourself the same affection you're capable of giving someone else, and you'll move mountains.